KISSD 2

KETAMINE CONFIDENTIAL

ROBERT C HIEMSTRA, MD

ISBN 979-8-952030-32-9 (softcover)
ISBN 979-8-952030-34-3 (hardcover)
ISBN 979-8-952030-33-6 (ebook)

Printed in the United States of America.

TABLE OF CONTENTS

PROLOGUE

The National Ketamine Depression Dilemma

At this moment in history, psychiatry is at a major crossroads in its approach to mental health. For the past 20 years psychiatry has been battling opponents, suppressing superior agents and generally trying to define a place for itself in a world that has changed in ways that it simply hadn't predicted. For psychiatry, the focus of that change has been the steady intrusion of ketamine into its confused world of SSRI and SNRI-treated depression. This is a world defined by attachment to money generated by SSRIs that are in turn being defined by the phenomenally effective antidepressant ketamine.

But this is much more than a battle of brands. The huge monies involved are rivaled in importance only by the massive population affected. This story is not simply one of large numbers. There is a horrible epidemic going on that is only barely being recognized, let alone defined.

Every segment of the population is seeing an increase in anxiety and depression, and in our teen population - the iGens - the percentage of the involved population may be massive. In my office I query every teen with questions relating to how many of their peers are afflicted. The estimates are seldom below 50% and oftentimes reach up to 90%. These are not professionals, but depression of this variety is hard to hide. In any case, it would seem to deserve far more attention than it is getting, if for no other reason than to offer solace to a frightened public.

Is psychiatry even looking? Of course, they must be, but with the look-the-other-way response that they've given to the miracle cures of ketamine - a product that they know works – mustn't we ask, "Is there a monied interest prompting you, psychiatry, to look in some other direction while whatever it is that is this dark, malignant, and as yet undefined Pied Piper gobbles our children?"

This question of abandonment of one's medical charge by an entire medical specialty is the topic of a jarring and disquieting article in the

October 31, 2019 issue of the New England Journal of Medicine, the world's most prestigious medical journal. I very literally gasped as I read the article, undoubtedly a product of my near miss in almost selecting psychiatry as a specialty more than 40 years ago.

The article makes the claim that "over the past half-century, biologic research has come to largely replace all other forms of psychiatric research - psychosocial, cultural, public health, and community - which have been marginalized in spite of the useful knowledge these fields provide for everyday care of patients in prevention of mental illness... Biologic knowledge is foundational to good psychiatry, but we believe that misapprehension of its limitations is stunting the field from within and subjecting it to manipulation from without by corporate administrative interests that, intentionally or not, strive to benefit from a falsely simplified, deterministic formulation of mental illness and its treatment."`[1]

The article quotes historian Anne Harrington proposing that "psychiatry limit its scope to severe, mostly psychotic disorders. 'Make no mistake, today one is hard-pressed to find anyone knowledgeable who believes that the so-called biological revolution of the 1980s made good on most or even any of its therapeutic and scientific promises.'"[2]

On every level, this is big stuff. There are violations of Hippocratic oaths buzzing around the heads of the majority of mental health patients in America.

Shouldn't these loud, obtrusive, and endlessly hurtful violations be not only resisted, but pointed out? If I keep quiet about the ongoing, constant, negative consequence of continuing to use SSRIs as first- order drugs, aren't I also guilty?

I think so.

And don't forget, that Pied Piper feasting on our your kids.

---

1 *Caleb Gardner and Arthur Kleinman, "Medicine and the Mind — The Consequences of Psychiatry's Identity Crisis," New England Journal of Medicine 381:18 (October 31, 2019): 1697-1699.*

2 *"Psychiatry's Identity Crisis," 1698.*

PREFACE

A Ketamine Step Is Taller Than the Sky

As physicians we enjoy the messed trappings of the scientist and, like that scientist, we rely upon data to give structure to our healing approaches for the sick and wounded. This work is defined by data from two quite different sources. The world of psychiatry has met with much disappointment and frustration over the past 30 years as it has been forced to recognize its inability to identify the necessary biological markers to qualify as a science. At the same time, psychiatry has suffered the revelations of marked ineffectiveness of its primary pharmacologic tools, the SSRIs and the SNRIs. Further, the entire conceptual structure of psychiatric maladies—with its dependence upon simple lists of symptoms for diagnosis—has shown little correlation with genuine, reproducible disease. This is discussed in the lengthy Chapter 2, which is based on Anne Harrington's major work, The Mind Fixers.[3]

The other significant data source concerning us here is that from the data collected at my clinic, Ketamine for Depression Salt Lake City (Ketamine SLC). With this data we have been able to define a ketamine dosage and consequent depression-free interval length that provides an actual standard of care to be pursued by ketamine practitioners. The original promise of ketamine suggested that the protocol administration of ketamine of 0.5 mg/kg IV over 40 minutes in six treatments within 12 days would give a depression-reduced interval of 3 months. But this 3-month period was seldom if ever achieved at that minimal dosage.

That 3-month interval of reduced depression is, however, achievable at higher dosages. These higher doses require slightly more attention but are still below the threshold of defined "anesthesia." Though safely accessible,

3 *Anne Harrington, The Mind Fixers, (New York: W.W. Norton & Co., Inc., 2019): 271-276.*

that accessibility is temperamental. It cannot simply be charged into, full bull into the matador. We must be delicate, sympathetic and cognizant of the most mundane of obstacles keeping us from our goals. Unfortunately, the intravenous administration of ketamine comes with two very practical difficulties—to be discussed in greater detail later—that limit its use in maximizing this depression-reduced interval of 3 months.

First some key definitions:

The Response Rates

R1 = The initial PHQ-9 reading for a patient, or the collection of those readings for a clinic.

R2 = The post-ketamine series PHQ-9 reading, or the collection of post-ketamine series readings for a clinic.

R3 = The interval of positive PHQ-9 responses from R2—or a "booster" (to be defined)—to the return of depression = "PHQ-9 over time."

The "Holy Grail of Depression" = our goal in the world of ketamine = 3 months of reduced depression without any therapeutic drug level or side effects.

Ketamine SLC has developed a system of gradually increasing the tolerance to ketamine such that an adequate total dose of ketamine may be administered through a limited number of doses in a single day. The original total amount of ketamine in the formula I just gave is 3.0 mg/kg, which is insufficient for most people. Through trial and error, we know that 6.0 mg/kg will very often deliver the Holy Grail of Depression, so that is our soft, to-be-catered-to-the-patient dose that serves as our general target. That system of gradually increasing ketamine administration we have termed KISSD, an acronym.

KISSD—Ketamine Intramuscular Stepped System for Depression—is a stairway that guides both the patient and the provider with landmarks that are themselves the stuff of relief from depression, anxiety and post-traumatic stress disorder (PTSD). A ketamine step is an increasing dose in a series of increasing doses that moves toward a dosing structure that provides relief from the most disabling and painful malady known to humankind, depression.

1. A ketamine step has structure and texture that manifest from four parameters:

2. Ketamine's unvarying biologic half-life: a peak at 18 minutes and a readiness for another dose at 30 minutes.
3. The progressive dose is defined by the biology and attitude of mind leading to the decision at each step. The patient constantly participates.
4. The "set" of set and setting, which refers to attitude or state of mind.
5. The "setting," which defines the world in which we sit, the physical world around us.

Whereas a ketamine step is always a half-hour long, its height can be shorter than one's socks or taller than the sky, lower than an anthill or higher than the moon. Such is the measurelessness of dissociation, the 10,000 shapes of psychedelia or the bigger-than-the-sky nature of the happily expanded mind.

We follow and come to know every step of ketamine to whatever height or depth it takes us, but the gong that marks the end of the 30 minutes and the step also marks a time of assessment and of decision for both the patient and the guide.

With that final gong we come to know a measure of dissociation that is psychedelia so that we may name a place to put our feet for the next step, which is a shaped dose of ketamine that moves us toward that greatest of goals, the Holy Grail of Depression.

This Holy Grail is the one hundred days of freedom that awaits us at the top of the ketamine stepped stairway. The quest for this Holy Grail is the great quest of the hero in search of the one true destiny that is the knowledge of self, for there is a measure of fear awaiting this very genuine explorer. The freedom from depression that is this Holy Grail of Depression offers all of this, for it is the offer of normalcy to unlivable disease, of cure to ultimate mental contagion, and of happiness to those in deepest despair.

SCIENTIFIC NOMENCLATURE AND THE STATISTICS OF DEPRESSION, ANXIETY AND PTSD.

With respect to nomenclature, standard approaches apply, though I do introduce the lateral habenula (LHb) and the lateral habenula burst mode (LHBM) in multiple chapters. Where the LHb and its LHBM have been shunned by Big Pharma and conventional psychiatry to the great detriment of their patients suffering from depression, anxiety and PTSD, their emphasis here comes as a product of each chapter's individual history but is maintained as a statement to underline their inappropriate historical exclusion as discussed in coming chapters.

Considering the stresses of the current pandemic as well as the steady inroads to depression carved by the cellphone among our teens, no one knows just how many are suffering, exactly who is suffering or how badly they are suffering. The question, "How many?" must recognize that prevalence defines how many will be afflicted during a given year, whereas the total number of citizens suffering during their lives will be significantly higher. Conventional statistics put depression at 5-15%, anxiety at 15-20% and PTSD at 5-10%. Mixed with that figure is the recognition that 12% of Americans are taking antidepressants.[4] Though they certainly overlap, these figures represent separate entities. Adding them together does give value in trying to understand the extent of the medical problem confronting ketamine, an agent found to be effective in treating all three conditions.

Recognizing the pandemic and current politics, I am taking the position that using the upper values of the numbers probably better describes the overall problem.

---

4 *Gary Greenberg, "Psychiatry's Incurable Hubris," The Atlantic (April 2019)13-14). BookBaby. Kindle Edition.*

For this paper I will assume the following general numbers, though I appreciate their dynamic nature:

Problem	General Prevalence	Approx. Number US
Depression	5-15%	20 million
Anxiety	15-20%	30 million
PTSD	5-10%	10 million

KISSD2:

Ketamine Confidential

Ketamine Confidential: A special Introduction for this rewrite of a book written early in my ketamine career. Much has changed as the world of depression has gained the ketamine that challenges so thoroughly the minimalist medicines of modern mental health. To underline the significance of these times as well as the always difficult to measure mood disorder of depression, I call a bit on Anthony Bourdain for help. Knowing of his personal trials with depression, including its role in his final departure, I'm sure that he would have much to add.

Anthony Bourdain's *Kitchen Confidential* pulled back the stainless-steel curtain on restaurant kitchens, revealing a world of risk, vanity, skill, desperation, and truth. It was a social book masquerading as a food book—less about nutrition or disease than about how people actually live and work when no one is watching.

KISSD2: Ketamine Confidential is inspired by that same act of exposure—but its subject is far darker, quieter, and vastly more lethal.

Food is something we all obsess over. We debate toxins, freshness, microbes, and moral sourcing. We teach children to fear bad fish and undercooked chicken. We worry, appropriately, about what we put into our bodies.

Depression, by contrast, kills silently.

It hides in bedrooms, back offices, dorm rooms, clinics, and smiling conversations. It is a disease with an extraordinarily low social profile despite its catastrophic human cost. Anxiety, depression, and PTSD disable tens of millions of Americans, yet they are routinely minimized, misdiagnosed, moralized, or monetized. Unlike foodborne illness, depression does not announce itself with vomiting or fever. It withdraws. It disguises itself as laziness, weakness, or personality. And when it finally kills, it often does so in a way that leaves no obvious fingerprints.

This book exists to expose that hidden world—and the professional failures that allow it to persist.

The Stealth Disease and the Stealth Failure

Depression is notoriously difficult to diagnose with certainty. There is no blood test, no scan, no culture plate. Its symptoms overlap uncomfortably with fatigue, grief, loss of motivation, and despair—states that medicine has too often dismissed as character flaws. That diagnostic ambiguity has created fertile ground for indifference, delay, and rationalization.

It has also created a convenient hiding place for professional misconduct.

When a psychiatrist offers warm reassurance while prescribing anything *except* the most effective available treatment—when that avoidance is driven not by science, but by money—that physician is not practicing caution. He is violating the Hippocratic Oath in its most fundamental form.

Ketamine is not new. It is not fashionable. It is not patentable. And that, more than any safety argument, explains psychiatry's resistance to it. Ketamine threatens the SSRI/SNRI business model precisely because it works—rapidly, predictably, and at scale.

To suppress an effective treatment for a deadly disease in order to preserve revenue streams is not merely unethical. It is cruel.

Why the Food Metaphor Matters

Food poisoning is common. It is unpleasant. It occasionally kills. But it is visible, finite, and culturally understood. A bad meal comes and goes. The danger is acknowledged, discussed, regulated, and feared appropriately.

Depression does none of these things.

For every completed suicide, there are hundreds—perhaps thousands—of people living in quiet psychological ruin. Their suffering is invisible, self-reinforcing, and isolating. Depression feeds on itself. It erodes hope, distorts identity, and whispers convincing lies about worthlessness and escape.

And yet, as a society, we worry more about a questionable oyster than about the person sitting next to us who has silently considered suicide.

That mismatch—between attention and harm—is the moral failure this book confronts.

Ketamine and the Obligation to Act

No one fully understands depression, anxiety, or PTSD. Their evolutionary origins, neurobiological triggers, and precise mechanisms remain elusive. What we *do* know is this: when ketamine is used correctly, it can reliably interrupt the depressive state and restore functional emotional range.

At Ketamine for Depression, Salt Lake City, the KISSD protocol has produced a result unmatched in modern psychiatry:

Approximately 70% of patients achieve at least 100 days of complete freedom from depression.

That fact alone creates an obligation.

When an effective tool exists, withholding it is no longer ignorance—it is choice. And when that choice is driven by financial incentive, institutional self-protection, or bureaucratic cowardice, the resulting harm is not abstract. It is measured in lives diminished and lives lost.

What This Book Is—and Is Not

KISSD: Ketamine Intramuscular Stepped System for Depression was written as a practical manual for physicians and patients—a cookbook for safe, effective ketamine treatment, accompanied by essays describing the emerging world around it.

KISSD2: Ketamine Confidential goes further.

It includes the ketamine "cookbook," but it also documents eight years of experience inside a system that responded to success not with curiosity, but with hostility. These essays trace the evolution of a profoundly dysfunctional relationship with regulators, academic psychiatry, and professional institutions more concerned with control than care.

This is not a grievance memoir. It is a case study in how effective medicine threatens entrenched interests—and how those interests retaliate.

Part II — New Chapters

XV. A Scale of Human Happiness

A moment of clinical revelation: the first realization that ketamine could not only reduce depression, but reliably avert suicide. Written early in the clinic's life, before regulatory interference, this chapter captures the raw astonishment of discovering that something long believed untreatable suddenly was not. It is unpolished, urgent, and intentionally so—because history rarely announces itself politely.

XVI. Depression's Greatest Lie

An examination of the most destructive deception depression tells both patients and physicians: that nothing else is possible. This chapter explores how diagnostic uncertainty, therapeutic inertia, and professional timidity conspire to preserve suffering under the guise of prudence.

XVII. Ketamine, Power, and the Circularity of Influence

Using public controversy surrounding high-profile figures as a lens, this chapter examines how ketamine collides with cultural power, media narratives, and fear-based storytelling. The medicine is less on trial here than society's discomfort with rapid relief from despair.

XVIII. Grievances Against a Licensing Authority

A factual, unsentimental portrait of regulatory dysfunction. Prepared originally for legal review, this chapter documents how bureaucratic mechanisms can be weaponized to neutralize effective physicians when evidence fails to justify punishment.

XIX. The Corporatization of a Physician

The final chapter in the conflict: a measured but unflinching response to institutional revisionism. It confronts the quiet normalization of professional cruelty and asks whether medicine can still recognize courage when it threatens revenue.

KISSD2: Ketamine Confidential argues a simple proposition: when depression can be treated, failing to treat it is no longer an error—it is a moral act.

And morality, once exposed, does not retreat quietly.

PART I

The World of Ketamine and Depression

I began this short book as a guide to the clinical practice of the treatment of depression with ketamine. This practice is, by the very nature of ketamine and the current scheme of medical politics surrounding it, a relatively focused entity. The mental health establishment ignores this mighty drug and the benefits it could bestow upon its patients; the fact that this immeasurably valuable drug is being ignored and suppressed makes this clinic not only possible, but critically necessary if these ignored patients are to find relief.

I assert many times in this work that ketamine will one day be seen to be at least as influential as Thorazine, the wonder drug of the 1950s that set the stage for the pharmaceutical industry's takeover of psychiatry. The manner of the suppression of this most profound mental entity is only now being appreciated.

The history of psychiatry, whether deep or recent, is not the necessary stuff of the clinic. But history plays a role here. After all, it is psychiatry's failure to fulfill its treatment promises—let alone its ability to define world of mental disease in scientifically acceptable modes—that now defines the world of ketamine. We know now that psychiatry's pharmacology for depression has succeeded by diversion, by changing the personality, not actually treating the depression. We know that psychiatry's science as presented in the Diagnostic and Statistical Manual of Mental Disorders (DSM) series is simply **NOT** science. With SSRIs demonstrating an effectiveness in treating depression of only 18% of a sugar pill, ketamine is all there is. Ketamine represents the only currently effective pharmacologic therapy for depression on the market.[5]

Chapter 2 is, then, the most important chapter in Part I. This chapter provides a perspective that gives validity to the nature of the dysfunction in

5 *Harrington, Mind Fixers, 262–265*

psychiatry. Consciousness and mind are mysterious, probably quantum phenomena, that are as far beyond our comprehension of their intimate science now as I write in 2021 as they were one hundred years ago during the emergence of Freud. To understand the degree of our current almost willful cluelessness, a tour of those times and their beliefs gives perspective. I minimally provide that as a windup to the great irony of psychiatry's current position—namely, the suppression of ketamine—a pharmaceutical described in the journal Nature as "arguably the most important advance in the field of psychiatry in the past half century."[6]

The great irony here is not simply that ketamine is a hugely effective drug when used for depression, but that psychiatry is suppressing it at a time when it is giving up on its fevered quest of the past 70 years to be a valid science, and ketamine could provide the science to give psychiatry the very validity it craves. The lateral habenula (LHb), our brain organ of despair, induces depression in a properly triggered mind by way of the lateral habenular burst mode (LHBM). The above- mentioned Nature article provides all the science needed to allow psychiatry to strut the robes of science that it has sought since first glimpsing the possibility in the days of Emil Kraepelin.[7]

Where the intentions of Chapter 2 are to underline the fundamental lack of science in the structure of psychiatry and the lack of effectiveness in its pharmacology, Chapters 4 and 5 redirect us from the idea that depression is an error, that it is a simple mistake of metabolism or genetics. This approach or attitude is familiar to us all in the concept of the chemical imbalance, which came to us with the flawed concept of the catecholamine hypothesis of affective disorders, coined in 1965.[8]

We have been rebalancing that nonexistent buggy wheel for 60 years and have yet to measure one genuine wobble.

Chapter 3 is a cautionary tale of the consequences of pulling the tails of Big Pharma and its perennial lackey, academic psychiatry, for they are as bulky and formidable as they are clueless and corrupt. Big Pharma speaks preferentially to big money. Depression is at least in part inherited, favoring females three to one, and we are seeing a national

6 *Yan Yang, Yihui Cui, Kangning Sang, Yiyan Dong, Zheyi Ni, Shuangshuang Ma, and Hailan Hu, "Ketamine blocks bursting in the lateral habenula to rapidly relieve depression," Nature Vol 554 (15 February 2018): 317–322.*

7 *Yang, "Ketamine blocks bursting in the lateral habenula," 317–322.*

8 *Harrington, Mind Fixers, 200–201.*

surge in anxiety and depression that seems to focus on teens in a way that suggests vulnerabilities to social media, cellphones and even authoritarian rule. There is far more than a simple chemical imbalance going on.

Chapter 4 defines many of the varieties of depression and their origins, and then describes their biologic structure, which is essentially that of a brain state defined by evolutionarily acquired networks of neurons. Read this chapter to know you do not make your own biggest decisions.

Chapter 5 pushes this theme of acquired, selected-for behavior in defining not only depression but also our sense of hierarchy, taste for money and hunger for varieties of sexual expression and dominance.

Part I gives a big-picture perspective—both of the field of psychiatry as a branch of medicine—and of depression as a thing of choice, where the decision to adopt the mode of behavior that is depression is seen as a response of mind to its own imperatives as it reacts to the greater universe in which it is embedded.

CHAPTER 1

The History of Ketamine and Depression

We are so lonely, and we are getting more so every day.

In a Time Magazine special edition on mental illness, 20,000 American adults reported in a recent Ipsos survey that half of them were painfully lonely some or all of the time, while one in four adults deny having friends or family members who really understand them.[9] For many of these people, upon the TV has been bestowed the ultimate accolade of best friend.

In Asia between 1992 and 2008 a study showed that loneliness in older folks doubled from 16% to 30%. American teens report feeling socially isolated 10% of the time.

Statistics show that mortality goes up 26% with loneliness, placing suffered social isolation as a death-enhancing health risk approximately equivalent to smoking and obesity.

Loneliness probably exerts its health risk by way of inflammation which contributes to heart disease, cancer, diabetes and many other diseases. Being the social creatures that human beings are, living without regular contact with companions places them in a constant state of stress.

Our main social organ is the brain. Deprived of its fundamental sociality, its response is to go into a stress mode where it spews stress chemicals, alters signaling pathways, and enters into the stress-slide of anxiety that eventually triggers the black snake of the lateral habenula to produce the defining lateral habenular burst mode that is the primary source of depression.[10]

Loneliness and its stress are not evenly distributed among peoples in a given society. Loneliness seems to be associated with transitions, and

---

9 *"The Loneliness Epidemic." In Time Mental Health Special Edition, edited by Edward Felthenthal. (New York: Meredith Corporation, 2019): 16–21.*

10 *Yang, "Ketamine blocks bursting in the lateral habenula," 317–322.*

as such adolescents and those at retirement age are seeing especially high rates of anxiety and depression. And where teens have smartphones and social media to greatly enhance their statistical numbers of depression and anxiety, old folks have fewer children to keep them engaged, leaving them with high rates of "kinlessness" in a new digital world designed around being alone.

The latest nature magazine catalogs a progression of anxiety in research graduates that shows that currently 50 to 75% are suffering significant anxiety. In 2017, an American College Health Association survey involving more than 63,000 students, 61% claimed "overwhelming anxiety," while almost 40% claimed depression so great that it was difficult for them to function.[11]

In my own office, I query every teen that passes through. I consistently get estimates of 50 to 90% of their fellow students as suffering from depression and anxiety manifested as the currently typical reluctance to look one in the eye, speak rather than text, or leave one's bedroom.

And doctors are a part of the medical problem. At least 400 doctors a year commit suicide and, as is commonly acknowledged, that rate could be much larger owing to a kind of cover-up of respect that seems to attend physician suicide. Where doctors enter medical school with a depression rate reflecting the normal population at 4%, during internship the rate shoots up to 25%, and doctors apparently afford themselves little compassion or care; little treatment is available during the typical medical residency. "Half of all docs are burned out," says the Time magazine article.[12]

There is even a "secret sorrow" suggested at the core of celebrity life, as evidenced by the recent Anthony Bourdain-Kate Spade suicides. Perhaps no place is safe from whatever fundamental menace currently afflicts us.

If this is a valid reflection of the disease, and most caregivers that I've spoken to think that it is, we have a WWII level of concern here - and we don't even know who the enemy is.

Houston, LA, Omaha, New York, St. George, Atlanta – we have a problem.

---

11 *Katie Reilly, "Depression on Campus," in Time Mental Health Special Edi- tion, edited by Edward Felthenthal (New York: Meredith Corporation, 2019): 28.*

12 *Mandy Oaklander, "A Toll on Doctors," in Time Mental Health Special Edi- tion, edited by Edward Felthenthal (New York: Meredith Corporation, 2019): 34.*

But in the October 2019 New England Journal of Medicine, in an article entitled "Medicine and the Mind - The Consequences of Psychiatry's Identity Crisis," it is revealed that psychiatry has significantly and dangerously departed from the practice of practical psychiatry.

"Psychiatry finds itself plagued by over-prescription of psychiatric medication for a large segment of the population; abandonment and incarceration of people with chronic, severe mental illness; and an increasingly unwieldy diagnostic system of overlapping symptom checklists. Psychiatry should be uniquely positioned to help with this crisis through example, scholarship, and consultation, yet the field seems to have largely abandoned its social, interpersonal, and psychodynamic foundations, with little to show for the sacrifices. There is substantial unmet need for psychiatric treatments and care for children and adolescents, and the emergence of mental health as a priority in the global health arena has increased the role of psychiatry in both international settings and the poorest populations in the United States."[13]

In the article, historian Anne Harrington suggests, "that psychiatry limit its scope to severe, mostly psychotic disorders."

What? Limit your scope in the middle of an epidemic? Well, if you aren't doing any good, perhaps it is best not to participate. Few professionals believe that SSRIs are any kind of valid answer to mild to moderate depression, anxiety or PTSD – SSRIs are clinically effective only in the upper limits of severity. The Star*D trial is often quoted as an example of SSRI antidepressant efficacy and, as such, is rich testimony to their lack of effectiveness.

For the last 15 to 20 years of ketamine's presence on the stage of depression therapy, there has been a self-serving rule in psychiatry that ketamine should be recognized as a potential treatment only after having failed two or more SSRIs. This rule has always been fraught with self-interest and has kept tens of thousands of suffering patients from a reasonable expectation of relief from treatment with ketamine. Now, evidence has never really been at the core of the constraints placed on ketamine; the problem has always been about money and the billions that big Pharma yearly takes in from SSRIs that are doing more damage than good. With Esketamine's donation of respectability to ketamine

---

13 Gardner, "Psychiatry's Identity Crisis," 1698.

as the public grants warranted acceptability, that hurtful, Hippocratic oath-defying barrier to treatment should be changed to:

New Rule: no SSRI should ever be initiated before a failed trial of ketamine.

With suicides, anxiety, depression and PTSD all at record levels and increasing in ways that we simply don't understand, ketamine is a miracle drug perched at a perfect moment in history to make a difference. To remain attached to SSRIs is to be described by Upton Sinclair's most famous quote: "It is difficult to get a man to understand something when his salary depends on his not understanding it."[14]

On this note, I would assert that administration of an SSRI before ketamine constitutes a fundamental violation of one's Hippocratic oath if that physician is fully knowledgeable of the actions of these drugs; reading the quoted Nature article should direct any physician to a proper mode of action.[15]

"The discovery of the rapid antidepressant effects of the NMDAR antagonist ketamine is arguably the most important advance in the field of psychiatry in the past half-century."

"Ketamine blocks bursting in the lateral habenula to rapidly relieve bursting."

Nature Feb 15, 2018

But I am not here to get lost in pointing fingers at vulnerabilities in others adherence to their Hippocratic oaths; there's just not enough time. People are dying and suffering more every day as a consequence of this failing.

Ketamine can make a big difference - and is making a difference - on the few that are able to experience its benefits. But less than 1% of the population that could benefit from ketamine has come to know its joys; its acceptance is growing and its potential for making a difference on the planet is enormous.

Within the ketamine world there is much variation in administration of the drug, accessibility to treatment, and effectiveness of the drug, which is a product of the first two factors. Money has been a big factor in accessibility where price keeps the medicine from those who need it.

---

14 *Upton Sinclair, The Jungle, (Double day, Page & Co. February 26, 1906).*

15 *Yang, "Ketamine blocks bursting in the lateral habenula," 317–322.*

Where the ketamine itself seldom costs more than one or two dollars per treatment, a treatment session typically costs from $400 to $800, and there are typically six treatments per therapeutic series.

Ketamine for Depression is the cheapest ketamine in America for two reasons:

1. The initial price per session of $300 where at least two injections are administered each session.
2. The typical six injections of a series are condensed to only one, so that the price is effectively *1/6 that of a typical full series.*

In the world of mental health medicines, no individual medicine has ever been discovered by looking for it. As recounted in Jeffrey Lieberman's sober book on psychiatry, "Shrinks," every psychiatric medicine in popular use is a product of serendipity. SSRIs are a kind of twisted testimonial to this observation in that we don't know how they work, or even if they do work, but we can make as many copycat versions of them as we like.

And remember that we are apparently in an epidemic situation where, despite our current treatment regimens, depression, anxiety and PTSD are all increasing. We need to figure out ways to address this problem in numbers far greater than we've ever considered and we must do it with fewer doctors per patient population than we've had before. Also, as mentioned earlier, the doctors are depressed, too.

Ketamine for Depression Salt Lake City is currently in the running for the busiest ketamine for depression clinic in America which, in the midst of an epidemic, is a valuable asset; this clinic has treated over 2,000 patients for whom we have administered over 7,800 treatments. What makes this possible is the development of a "stepped" system of ketamine administration where the dose is increased to meet patient needs in a graduated fashion that utilizes patient participation in the decision-making. Dosages, ancillary medicines, and continuance of care are are at least in part communal decisions. This system, acronymed to "KISSD," or *Ketamine Intramuscular Stepped System for Depression*, will be defined and discussed in later chapters.

As Lieberman's book suggests, we are *very unlikely to find a replacement for ketamine, or something that is better, anytime in the next 20 years*. One might argue that the 20 year figure is overly pessimistic, but optimism would require dealing not just with the book, "Shrinks," but with the above earlier assertion that understanding the mind is even farther away now than it was 50 years ago when ketamine was invented. That we have many more tools is certain and will always be exciting, but that the landscape has gotten far more obscure and evermore less accessible can be denied only at great peril.

"In many ways, the unknown continent of the
mind looms even larger now than it did in Jaspers' day (100 years ago) -
a reality that is both humbling and inspiring."
N ENGL J Med October 31, 2019

Where we have very little understanding of the actual mechanisms of SSRIs, ketamine is quite another story. We will now discuss some of ketamine's multiple modes of efficacy before describing the KISSD system of stepped ketamine for depression.

This data—though certainly disturbing—was known; we have noted an increase in disturbed teens for at least the past decade. What was concerning about this event was that recent internal polling from Facebook, recently leaked to the public, allegedly duplicated the results, but had been reported by Facebook as having been positive and healthful.[16]

Within the world of depression there is much variation in the administration and accessibility to the drug, which in turn defines its societal effectiveness. Money has been a crucial factor in accessibility to ketamine, where price often keeps the medicine from those who need it. Where ketamine itself seldom costs more than $1 or $2 per treatment, a treatment session typically costs $400 to $800, and there are usually six treatments per therapeutic series.

Ketamine for Depression SLC offers the cheapest ketamine in America for two reasons: (1) The initial price per session is $300 where at least two injections are administered each session. (2) The typical six injections of a series are eventually condensed to only one "booster" every three months, so that the effective price drops to one–sixth that of a typical full series.

In the world of mental health medicines, no individual mental health medicine has ever been discovered by looking for it. As recounted

---

16 *John Della Volpe, "Instagram has negatively impacted social relationships, according to new youth poll," www.msnbc.com/morningjoe. (September 20, 2021).*

in Jeffrey Lieberman's sobering book on psychiatry, Shrinks, every psychiatric medicine in popular use is a product of serendipity.[17]

The SSRIs, which constitute psychiatry's mainstay of pharmacologic depression care, are a kind of twisted testimonial to this observation in that we do not know how they work, or even if they do work, but we can make as many copycat versions of them as we like.

We must remember also that—in addition to a Covid pandemic—we are in the midst of a mental health epidemic where—despite our current treatment regimens—depression, anxiety and PTSD are all increasing. We need to figure out ways to address this problem in numbers far greater than we have ever considered before, and we must do it with fewer doctors per patient population than we have had before. Also, as mentioned earlier, the doctors are depressed, too.

Ketamine for Depression SLC is currently in the running for the busiest ketamine–for–depression clinic in America which, during the pandemic, is a timely asset. This clinic has treated more than $3,000 patients for whom we have administered more than $11,000 treatments. What makes this possible is the development of a "stepped" system of ketamine administration where the dose is increased to meet patients' needs in a graduated fashion that utilizes patient participation in the decision–making. Dosages, ancillary medicines and continuance of care are at least in part communal decisions. This system, termed the **Ketamine Intramuscular Stepped System for Depression (KISSD)**, is defined and discussed in later chapters.

As Lieberman's book suggests, we are very unlikely to find a better replacement for ketamine within the next 20 years. One might argue that the 20-year figure is overly pessimistic, but optimism would require dealing not just with the book Shrinks, but also with my earlier assertion that the mind is even farther away from a fundamental understanding of its nature now than it was 50 years ago when ketamine was invented. That we have many more tools is certain and will always be exciting, but that the landscape has gotten far more obscure and evermore less accessible can be denied only at great peril. "In many ways, the unknown continent of the mind looms even larger now than it did in Jasper's day (100 years ago)—a reality that is both humbling and inspiring."[18]

---

17 Jefferey A. Lieberman, M.D., with Ogi Ogas, Shrinks The Untold Story of Psychiatry, (New York: Little, Brown and Company, March 2015): 184, 294, 310.

18 Gardner, "Psychiatry's Identity Crisis," 1698.

Where we have very little understanding of the actual mechanisms of SSRIs, ketamine is quite another story. In Part II I return to the medical intricacies of ketamine. We will now go to history for larger perspectives on psychiatry's evolution and the fundamental imperatives of humankind, a quite vicious story.

CHAPTER 2

The History of Psychiatry and Its Quest for Science

"As long as the research community takes the DSM to be a bible, we'll never make progress … Biology never read that book."[19]

The terms "mind" and "consciousness" define frontiers that in a medical sense science has yet to effectively enter, but psychiatry's failure to launch was not for wont of intention or effort. For the past 70 years psychiatry has asserted an intention to be scientific, to be directed by biologic markers that define mentation as they allow statistical evaluation, understanding and then manipulation of that mental biology. But rather than adapting to science and its truths, psychiatry chose to sit back and watch as the entire DSM system of cataloging disease fell progressively apart in a kind of feet-of-clay irrelevance. During the same moments that psychiatry's major pharmaceutical weapons—the SSRIs and SNRIs—acquired their own versions of feet- of-clay irrelevance with a new recognition that their antidepression powers amounted to no more than 18% of a sugar pill, their adverse side effects were costing their pharmaceutical manufacturers billions in legal fees.[20]

With medically worthless tools, a bankrupt science and a morally corrupt bottom line, psychiatry would seem to have nowhere to go. But if the great minds of psychiatry would only open up their apex, science-questing brains, they could diagnose the sick before them, define scientifically valid biologic markers of mental disease and then treat that disease with the single most effective agent for anxiety, depression and PTSD ever recognized. Ketamine, the hottest psychiatric agent to hit

---

19 *Anne Harrington, The Mind Fixers, (New York: W.W. Norton & Co., Inc., 2019): 267.*

20 *Scott H. Podolsky, M.D., David Herzberg, Ph.D., and Jeremy A. Greene, M.D., Ph.D., "Preying on Prescribers (and Their Patients)—Pharmaceutical Mar- keting, Iatrogenic Epidemics, and the Sackler Legacy," New England Journal of Medicine Vol 380, no 19. (May 9, 2019): 1785–1787.*

the neurons of the afflicted since Thorazine, will save psychiatry from itself as it alters the depression, anxiety and PTSD that has taken over the planet.

This book is a story of ketamine's recent emergence into both psychiatry's and our nation's growing dysfunction.

In her exhaustive, colorful and insightful book, *The Mind Fixers: Psychiatry's Troubled Search for the Biology of Mental Illness*, Anne Harrington makes the historical case that psychiatry's high hopes for an imminent biological explanation of mind and mental function were not just misplaced, but with that failure of explanation would come the opportunistic predation of the world's citizenry by Big Pharma.[21] The key moment and event was the 1980s release of DSM-III, the American Psychiatric Association's (APA) manual of mental disease, which suggested science was about to penetrate the mysteries of mind and mental function such that men of medicine could understand and treat them as they did routinely in other specialties with every other organ of the body.

But it was not to be. Thirty-three years later, with the 2013 release of DSM-5, psychiatry recognized that the required biologic markers of science to define mental disease into genuine biologic, organic entities simply were not there. Harrington quotes Allen Francis where he asserts that the current DSM system of a "checklist" approach to diagnosis allowed money-oriented Big Pharma to predate the afflicted citizenry with "false positive 'epidemics'" and harmful excessive treatment.[22]

Harrington quotes Stephen Hyman, a former National Institute of Mental Health (NIMH) director who discussed the mental health world in 2013, as saying that no one could have anticipated such a decisive downward spiral in 1980 when the original authors of DSM-III "were real heroes at the time … They chose a model in which all psychiatric illnesses were represented as categories discontinuous with normal." But, he went on, they were "totally wrong in a way that couldn't have been imagined. So, in fact, what they produced was an absolute scientific nightmare. Many people … get five diagnoses—but they don't have five diseases—they have one underlying condition."[23]

---

21 *Harrington, Mind Fixers, 249.*

22 *Harrington, Mind Fixers, 268.*

23 *Harrington, Mind Fixers, 269.*

For 13 years Thomas Insel followed Stephen Hyman as the NIMH director, but he finally left the agency disappointed and disillusioned. He made the following comment upon his exit:

> "I spent 13 years at NIMH really pushing on the neuroscience and genetics of mental disorders, and when I look back on that I realize that while I think I succeeded in getting lots of really cool papers published by cool scientists at fairly large costs—I think $20 billion—I don't think we moved the needle in reducing suicide, reducing hospitalizations, or improving recovery for the tens of millions of people who have mental illness. I hold myself accountable for that."[24]

In getting to scientific humility with respect to brain, mind and mental function, examining the history of psychiatry gives us limited insight into the unique way both interact with elements of society to produce this current moment. Harrington roughly defines nine historical entities as follows, with "The Instructive Case of 'Dr. C.'" coming from my own medical experience:

1. The 19th-century Mental Hospital.
2. Anatomical Research Programs.
3. Hysteria and Neurasthenia.
4. Shock and Surgical Treatments.
5. Neo-Freudians.
6. Biological Psychiatry.
7. Inventing Neurochemistry.
8. Psychopharmacology in Crisis.
9. Arthur Sackler's Advertising.
10. The Instructive Case of "Dr. C."

In what follows I briefly discuss a few of these histories for perspective, but the meat of this chapter occurs in its final five pages. For those less historically oriented, please move forward to those last pages and their summary conclusions, which set up the portrait of psychiatry that is important here.

---

24 Harrington, Mind Fixers, 269.

The 19th-Century Mental Hospital

Bedlam, originally a London hospital called St Mary Bethlehem that became the namesake for the hundreds of institutions like it, was essentially a place to keep the unmanageably insane out of the way. Early management systems were as creative as they were cruel and clueless, a reflection of those times.

Beliefs regarding the origins of mental illness leaned mostly toward blaming past experiences as the mind-fouling agents. In this limited context, a rest at the institution might provide a restorative and therapeutic respite for a person suffering from a routine level of stress, where the next patient might be afflicted with—unknown, of course, to the medical minds of the day—a decompensated schizophrenia that would keep her at the facility for the rest of her life.

These institutions were crude, of course, but they accepted a role we largely shirk today. We, as a society in the United States, once utilized a vaguely similar system of state hospitals that managed our unmanageable people, which are made up largely of patients suffering from schizophrenia. A combination of overestimating the accomplishments of Thorazine, neo-Freudians' hope that these newly released patients might lend themselves to psychotherapy and thoughts of tax containment at the state level resulted in the closure of these institutions. The consequence was the release of most incarcerated patients, who would then soon become the nameless homeless currently ever-present on most of our public streets.

Medical practitioners in these facilities were historically termed alienists. The American Psychiatric Association (APA) grew from this type of organization.

Anatomical Research Programs

Most early thinking on the origins of mental problems held the brain responsible. The contention was that if the brain really was responsible, we should be able to see anatomic changes in the brains of concern consistently reflected in the mental health problems observed during active life. Dissection was therefore the key to affirming diagnoses, which meant that after the patient was diagnosed, the anatomist essentially lost interest until the patient died and made himself and his brain available for dissection.

This anatomist became known as a "brain spot man" and came to be heavily criticized for keeping the patient distant by the physician in the asylum—who was known as a "brain twist man"—a reference to the presumed twisting of normal mind by experience. These "brain spot men" would later evolve into our modern neurologists—whereas "brain twist men" were made up primarily of Freudians, degeneration- oriented healers and biological psychiatrists—though the distinctions between these entities during those times were not nearly so clearly drawn as we now recognize them.

Hysteria and Neurasthenia

Hysteria, railway brain and railway spine comprised vague, undefined mental entities that could be altered by suggestion and were the focus of most healers. "Mental degeneration" was a term often thrown about but seldom recognized in any concrete form; if a mind was viewed as weird, or even just stupid, it was fodder for being deemed a product of degeneration.

Sigmund Freud entered the picture during these times by being the first to differentiate genuine neurologic disease from hysteria by simple observation of symptoms. Harrington quotes his stunning article, "Some Points for a Comparative Study of Organic and Hysterical Motor Paralysis," where he recognized that hysterical patients suffer from reminiscences where their medical "symptoms are the remnants and the memory symbols of certain (traumatic) experiences." When memory prompts the symptomatology, a "bum" leg that is a product of hysteria will operate very differently than one paralyzed by genuine traumatic disease.[25]

Where the term "psychotherapy" had originally been applied to any procedure meant to positively affect mental health, in Freud's shaping of his expansive theory of mental disease—replete with his focus on dreams, repressed sexuality and the unconscious—psychoanalysis acquired a definition unique to his perspective.

Shock and Surgical Treatments

Tertiary syphilis was for many years known as general paralysis of the insane, or GPI. Penicillin had not yet reduced its presence at all levels

---

25 *Harrington, Mind Fixers, 22–24.*

of society. From the discovery of the healing powers of malaria's fevers in 1887 until the introduction of penicillin 50 years later, malaria was used extensively at many facilities throughout the world for the treatment of syphilis.

The scientific establishment at this time thought that all psychoses—whether from schizophrenia, Freudian stresses or GPI—shared a single origin until the demonstration of the syphilis spirochete in the brain of a GPI-suffering patient displayed dramatically that infectious disease could cause psychoses. This was a big moment, and it gave Freud and his theory's dependence upon interpersonal conflict much pause.

Insulin was discovered in the 1920s. Described as young and ambitious, Manfred Sakel was a Viennese clinician who claimed near-miraculous responses of schizophrenics to his insulin shock therapy. As expensive as it was ineffective, this therapy is no longer utilized, though it saw a vogue that lasted years.

Metrazol shock treatment was performed under the assumption that schizophrenia could be altered by epileptic seizures. The basic theory was eventually proven untrue and metrazol soon disappeared.

Electroconvulsive treatment (ECT) was cheap, easily available and moderately effective for depression—though not for the schizophrenics for whom it was originally developed—and is still used today. Memory loss is the most significant complaint regarding its use. Comparative studies show electroconvulsive treatment to be approximately half as effective as ketamine for depression, but always with memory loss and whatever other brain changes memory loss implies.[26]

Lobotomy, earning the Nobel Prize for Egas Moniz, is very simply a horror story starring Walter Freeman and his accomplice James Watts as they toured America icepicking the frontal lobes of the famous and the never to be known or heard from again. The appearance of chlorpromazine in 1954—often described as a chemical lobotomy—essentially ended its use, but not for years and after many hundreds, if not thousands, of never-to-be-reversed icepick lobotomies.

The Neo-Freudians

Freud gave us the construct of the unconscious, which is both valid

---

26 Stephen Hyde, "Ketamine for Depression," Xlibris, 2015, 52.

and valuable, but he then filled it with the nonsense of Greek incest and constant blame. Harrington points out that "Freudian psychoanalysis offered something that neuroanatomy and even serology had failed to offer: a coherent causal explanation for disease that led logically to a strategy for treatment." She quotes Gregory Zilboorg's *1941 History of Medical Psychology*. "The symptoms generated by the cause, and the therapeutic agent revealing and removing the cause were combined in one succession of factors … It was this combination that made clinical psychopathology a true medical discipline for the first time."[27] (Italics from original quote.)

Distinctly nonbiological, Freudian psychiatry looks to relationships and their cause-and-effect nature. As such, there is always someone to blame, and the mother seems to have been most often available to mostly male psychiatrists. "Schizophrenogenic mothers" were described for many years as the primary perpetrators for sourcing schizophrenia, while "refrigerator mothers" earned many wagging fingers from accusatory psychiatrists as the culprits for spawning a horrid autism in the very children that those mothers loved most and were closest to.

Attacks from many sources on the very nature of disease occurred during these times, poet R. D. Laing famously among them. Psychiatrist Thomas Szasz portrayed mental disease in his book *The Myth of Mental Illness* as a "myth" that gave "license to self-identified professionals to infringe on the civil liberties of others." Psychologist and lawyer David L. Rosenhan asserted, "The view has grown that psychological categorization of mental illness is useless at best and downright harmful, misleading, and pejorative at worst. Psychiatric diagnoses, in this view, or in the minds of observers, are not valid summaries of characteristics displayed by the observed."[28]

Rosenhan went on to make his point by having eight sane people purporting to hear voices uttering the words "hollow" and "thud" present themselves to a psychiatric facility. The counterfeit patients demonstrated no other symptoms but were admitted to the hospital to be released within 9 to 52 days with a diagnosis of "schizophrenia in remission." Apparently, no psychiatrist realized they were not mentally ill, though patients at the facility were reported to have asserted, "You're

---

27 Harrington, Mind Fixers, 82.

28 Harrington, Mind Fixers, 125.

not crazy. You're a journalist or professor. You're checking up on the hospital." Doctors at another psychiatric facility took issue with the resulting paper and delivered a challenge to send those patients to their facility where, they claimed, the counterfeits would surely be recognized. The challenge was accepted and over a period of several weeks hospital staff members there identified forty-one "stooges," though Rosenhan had sent no phony schizophrenics. Rosenhan concluded, "It is clear that we cannot distinguish the sane from the insane in psychiatric hospitals."[29]

Insight into the fundamental nature of mental disease, or at least how psychiatry viewed mental disease, has been addressed many times in discussions of same-sex attraction pathology, or lack thereof. Homosexuality is on the lists for both *DSM-I* and *DSM-II*, during which time this "crime of gross indecency" was the target of painful "conversion therapies," social ostracism and simple definitions of crime. After much internal debate and public dispute relating to psychiatry as "an agent of social control," the APA voted in 1973 to remove homosexuality from its list of mental illnesses; homosexuality did not appear as a disease designation in *DSM-III*, the next manual.

This alteration of disease designation by vote was not the first questioning of the nature of mental disease, but it very publicly underlined the dispute as it exposed psychiatry's own lack of understanding on its most fundamental issue: what is, and what is not, mental disease.

Biological Psychiatry

Thomas Insel has spent many years at the nexus of the biological psychiatry question, which basically asks, "Are valid science and statistics behind this particular portrait of reality?" One of his many answers to the contrary, as recounted by Harrington, is as follows:

> "As long as the research community takes the DSM to be a Bible, we'll never make progress," he told a New York Times journalist. "Biology never read that book... NIMH will be reorienting its research away from DSM categories... To begin to develop a better system."[30]

---

29 Harrington, Mind Fixers, 126.

30 Harrington, Mind Fixers, 267.

Biological psychiatry had taken a major hit during the Progressive Era in the 1910s and 1920s as its eugenics morphed into elements later associated with Nazi atrocity. This negative association was at least part of the reason for the postwar emergence of Freudian psychiatry with its focus on mental hygiene (which included recognition of personalities especially susceptible to dictators), maladjustment, everyday efficiency and blame.

Insight into psychiatry's evolution and history of intention can be gleaned from a peek at the series of formal manuals that asserted what were perceived as mental diseases and their definitions. The Statistical Manual for the Use of Institutions for the Insane was first published in 1919 for census purposes and hospital record-keeping. This manual defined twenty-two diagnoses.

The first Diagnostic and Statistical Manual (DSM) was released by the APA in 1952. Directed by the new neo-Freudian leadership, it displayed a lack of concern for its contents attributable to the fact that Freudian psychiatrists believed these diagnoses to be secondary products of the actual and fundamentally more important Freudian conflicts going on deeper down. Research comparing the varied diagnoses from different psychiatrists on the same patient showed agreement only 30% of the time; 70% of the time, they disagreed. In any other branch of medicine, Harrington asserts, these superficially scientific results would be scandalous, but in psychiatry it barely registered a yawn.

DSM-II was published in 1968 and was a product largely of Freudian thought, though it was poised for change. The most notable single event during its reign was its dealing with homosexuality. The entity was listed as a disease, but it was a disease that showed nothing abnormal in that the pathology associated with homosexuality showed no statistical differences from that of heterosexuals. As mentioned elsewhere, the issue was settled by the distinctly nonscientific mode of a vote. By vote, homosexuality was moved from a disease category to one of normalcy.

DSM-III marks the high point of optimism for biological psychiatry. The year was 1980. The expunging of homosexuality, along with almost

all psychoanalytic language, suggested a scientific, objective, distinctly non subjective approach to mental disease. Rather than the freewheeling clinical interview where psychiatrists' minds wandered in the diagnostic forest waiting for a diagnosis to pop up, a system of checklists was to be utilized. The checklist system, it was hoped, would effectively substitute for the more scientific biologic markers that were then thought soon to follow. Robert Spitzer was the recognized agent behind this push; in 1980, when the APA approved *DSM-III*, he received a standing ovation. But the fulfillment of his optimism was again not to be.

DSM-IV was released in 1994 under the direction of Alan Francis. It had a few more diagnoses, but otherwise was a simple expansion of the conceptualization and hope that had begun earlier with *DSM-III*.

DSM-5 was a different story when the APA published it in 2013; its designation with a number rather than a roman numeral has been said to imply a vague negativity. Harrington notes that Alan Francis observed that the process for DSM-5 had "started with the grand ambition to provide a paradigm shift in psychiatric diagnoses, based initially on the identification of biological markers," but that goal had proven "clearly unattainable," so efforts were now underway to create new syndromes likely to result in diagnoses for more and more people who are not really sick—leading to the "false positive epidemics" with "harmful excessive treatments."[31]

The multiple quotes from Thomas Insel at the beginning of this section were a disappointing product of the appearance of *DSM-5* and the acceptance by the psychiatric scientific community that the biology of psychiatry was not yet suggested on any horizon—or visible in any future—despite remaining perceptible to its practitioners.

Inventing Neurochemistry

Historically, vapors and humors dominated most thinking on the origins of physical and mental disease. Puerperal sepsis—the first actual agent of disease to reveal itself in modern terms—was thought for centuries to have floated in through the window as a vapor rather than be an infectious agent freshly scraped from the good doctor's blood-crusted, foul-smelling apron, until Hungarian physician Semmelweiz taught doctors to wash their hands, and Pasteur grew from culture the germ responsible, *Streptococcus pyogenes*.

These toxic vapors had been thought of as lurking in dark corners everywhere, but humors were thought to be static internal fluids whose balance defined our dispositions and our mental diseases. Various proportions of black bile, yellow bile, phlegm and blood defined one

31 *Harrington, Mind Fixers, 268.*

person's happiness and another's shame. Hippocrates gets credit for their invention, but it was Shakespeare who nailed them onto our psyches.

Science has replaced those humors with the actual chemicals of our mental existence, but we are still trying to figure out on many neurologic levels exactly which chemical in which situation goes with which mental state. Understanding an individual emotion's history, for instance—its cause and effect on microscopic, individual neurons—is simply beyond us. And we have yet to figure out which mental state is a disease, and which one is important for happiness, or which mental state had a survival function during the Neolithic that we might consider valuable, and which could be dangerous to society in our current high-tech, power-enhancing world.

Otto Loewi discovered acetylcholine, adrenaline and noradrenalin in the 1920s. Two decades later, Maurice Rapport revealed important roles for 5-hydroxytryptamine, whose name was changed to serotonin by its parent pharmaceutical company, Upjohn. Then LSD came onto the scene and was recognized to have something to do with serotonin receptors in what was thought to be a kind of lock-and-key mechanism. Likewise, vague thoughts of an association of schizophrenia, serotonin and mysterious "Substance M" were entertained. Arvid Carlsson discovered the prominence of dopamine in the brain while studying serotonin and norepinephrine. Some relationship of dopamine to Parkinson's disease, the substantia nigra and basal ganglia was noted but not further defined.

Amphetamines, first utilized as decongestants in the 1930s, came to social prominence in the 1960s when the amphetamine psychosis noted in speed freaks was determined to be almost indistinguishable from bouts of intense schizophrenia. In this context, Seymour Kety announced in the Saturday Review that the days of the neo-Freudians were numbered. "There are now substantial indications," he said, "that serious mental illnesses derive from chemical, rather than psychological, imbalances." Though the origins of schizophrenia had not yet been uncovered, the disease was increasingly seen as organic— as biological in origin—as opposed to the "schizophrenogenic mother" origin of the disease postulated by neo-Freudians.

Depression, anxiety and PTSD are currently portrayed as diseases of stress. For the period from World War II until the early 1960s, depression was considered rare and merely derivative of more important processes. Psychoanalytically oriented psychiatrists did not use depression as a diagnostic category very often; anxiety was their big issue of concern, where depression symptoms were seen as lesser issues clouding the psychodynamic battles going on deeper down.[32]

"Psychotic depressive reaction" was the "melancholy" of Shakespeare, the "black bile" of his physician contemporaries, and the 1952 DSM category that came to be described as "endogenous depression." But depression was still considered rare and remained so until the invention of the first antidepressant.

Iproniazid was originally an antibiotic that killed the tubercle bacillus. But the drug also made sad people party-happy, as the many photos of hospital-gowned partying patients testified. And they did not need as much sleep as they had previously. To distinguish the drug from amphetamines, it was called a "psychic energizer." Iproniazid was a flawed drug, but the less-flawed imipramine came out as Tofranil, soon followed by the most successful tricyclic ever, amitriptyline or Elavil.

That Elavil was doing something was obvious. But what? The answer that worked for those times is an amazing piece of fluff that became institutionalized as the "catecholamine hypothesis of affective disorders," which in turn gave rise to another piece of seemingly eternal fluff, the "chemical imbalance."

In 1965 National Institutes of Health (NIH) psychiatrist Joseph Schildkraut published his best guess at the chemistry behind depression in the American Journal of Psychiatry, in an article entitled "The Catecholamine Hypothesis of Affective Disorders."[33] Discussions of "chemical imbalance" followed from the article and, as sales of tricyclic antidepressants skyrocketed, the recognition of depression as its own entity followed a similar pathway.

Depression had, in fact, become as familiar in the mental health world as the common cold, that specific homily apparently attaching itself to depression almost as if directed by the ancient, phlegm- focused Hippocrates.

In 1960 the Hamilton Depression Scale (HAM-D) was developed and gave figures to the despondency the public was experiencing. At the same time anxiety was recognized as related to depression. Cognitive behavioral therapy (CBT) evolved and proved itself more effective than

---

32 *Harrington, Mind Fixers, 184.*

33 *Harrington, Mind Fixers, 200.*

the tricyclics, an academic problem of sorts for biological psychiatry. The World Health Organization asserted during these times that as much as 20% of the population of the West exhibited symptoms of depression.

Then, in December 1987, Eli Lilly introduced fluoxetine or Prozac. By 1988 Prozac had become history's best-selling antidepressant and, by 1990, 1 million prescriptions a month were being written. The role of money in both diagnoses and treatment had begun.

But much more was going on than just alterations of what were thought to be depression and anxiety. In Peter Kramer's 1993 book *Listening to Prozac*, the concept of personality enhancement was introduced by following a depression and anxiety-challenged lady, Tess, as she evolved from office napkin to corporate shiv. Physicians suddenly found themselves responsible for lifestyle enhancement. This new field of "cosmetic psychopharmacology" asserted that "since you only live once, why not do it as a blonde, and why not as a peppy blonde?"[34]

For 20 years the mental health pharmaceutical industry took in billions as it pushed these complicated themes of how to address the stresses of modern times. But it was not all smooth sailing, and eventually the public came to realize that "SSRIs did not always work, they did not work forever, and taking them was not without risks."

The year 1980, as mentioned earlier, had seen the publishing of **DSM-III** as the apex moment of the high hopes of biological psychiatry. President George H. W. Bush declared 1990 to be the beginning of the "Decade of the Brain." Hugely impressive imaging technologies evolved and suggested direct and immediate insight into mental function. But a sobering quote from NIMH director Tom Insel recalled that "during the so-called Decade of the Brain, there was neither a marked increase in the rate of recovery for mental illness, nor a detectable decrease in suicide or homelessness, each of which is associated with the failure to recover from mental illness."[35]

Despite those parameters of failure, many things were going on. Mental health drugs were being used in quantities and to effects never dreamed of. The **medical model**, as opposed to the Freudian model, had become a common focus. Harrington makes clear that this adherence was not a product of medical success but rather of forces outside of medicine.

---

34 *Harrington, Mind Fixers, 213.*

35 *Harrington, Mind Fixers, 249.*

The following is, I believe, the most important single paragraph of Anne Harrington's especially important work:

"This new consensus, however, did not happen simply because everyone now 'believed' in the medical model, or because prescribing privileges were one of the few things that still allowed psychiatrists to assert their identities as physicians or because Freud the man and psychoanalysis as a movement continued in the 1980s to suffer an onslaught of steady blows to their reputations. All three of these factors

were true and relevant, but they were dramatically amplified by a fourth: by the late 1980s, a critical mass of clinicians and researchers had aligned their professional interests with the commercial interests of the pharmaceutical industry.[36]

Though intention remained strong, biological psychiatry did not move forward. The 1980 **Bayh-Dole Act** cultivated medical discovery by allowing individual scientists to take out patents using federal dollars, and advocacy groups such as the National Alliance on Mental Illness (NAMI) stood behind the medical model. But no biological markers were identified, and Harrington quotes a *Nature Review* article as describing those years as a "barren time for the discovery of novel drugs for psychiatric disorders, in particular those that could revolutionize disease treatment." At best, there were "incremental improvements to classes of drugs that had been in use since the 1950s and 60s."[37]

What made it all work and kept it going was **advertising**—lots of advertising. The Food and Drug Administration (FDA) agreed in 1997 to relax the **direct-to-consumer (DTC) advertising** of prescription drugs, which then exploded from $800 million in 1996 to $4.9 billion in 2007, with psychiatric drugs generating twice the revenue of all other prescription drugs. The revenues generated by that $4.9 billion reached a peak of $14 billion in 2008, a near tripling of invested monies in one year.[38]

But it was not all smooth sailing. In 2006, as a product of litigation against Eli Lilly and its antidepressant, antianxiety, anti-irritability, anti-insomnia drug **Zyprexa**, Eli Lilly paid $1.2 billion to settle lawsuits with some 28,500 people who claimed Zyprexa induced diabetes. Harrington

---

36 *Harrington, Mind Fixers, 249.*

37 *Harrington, Mind Fixers, 251.*

38 *Harrington, Mind Fixers, 251–2.*

also quotes Gardiner Harris and Alex Berenson in a *New York Times* article "Lilly Said to Be Near $1.4 Billion US Settlement," where doctors were to be persuaded "to prescribe Zyprexa to elderly nursing home patients and disruptive children, for whom the drug was not approved."[39]

Psychopharmacology in Crisis

Harrington discusses Marcia Angell, a former editor of the *New England Journal of Medicine*, and her book *The Truth about Drug Companies*, in which she describes the pharmaceutical industry as "in some ways like the Wizard of Oz—still full of bluster but now being exposed as something far different from its image." She describes Big Pharma as a "fast marketing machine" that benefited from government-funded research as it claimed monopoly rights on its products.[40]

Harrington describes a marketplace now filled with books portraying the psychopharmaceutical industry as a target of moral outrage. Medication-induced obesity, high blood sugar, diabetes, unpredictable personality changes and simple ineffectiveness dominate the complaint list, but the single greatest problem—the question at the core of an assumption of medical effectiveness—is the "**placebo effect problem**."[41]

This entity has effectively removed most of Big Pharma from the mental health pharmaceutical industry.

The determination and definition of a drug's effectiveness in abating depression came from evaluating that drug to assess its performance in comparison to either a placebo sugar pill or another drug whose known benefits have previously been quantified. Data from the pharmaceutical companies themselves were often not available or suggested ineffective results.

In 1998, to define the placebo effect with more exactness, psychologist **Irving Kirsch** used a unique meta-analytic method for his study. Kirsch determined initially that "75% of the improvement seen in people taking active medication could be attributed to the placebo effect." As Kirsch said in his report, they had "listened" for Prozac, but soon realized they were actually "hearing" placebo.[42]

---

39 Harrington, Mind Fixers, 259.

40 Harrington, Mind Fixers, 250.

41 Harrington, Mind Fixers, 262.

42 Harrington, Mind Fixers, 263.

Big Pharma was not happy and said so publicly, even asserting the studies were simply untrue. Kirsch then utilized the Freedom of Information Act to force the FDA to send all approval data related to the six most widely prescribed antidepressant drugs at that time: **Prozac, Paxil, Zoloft, Effexor, Serzone and Celexa**. Coming out in 2002, the results were hugely revelatory. First, only **43% of the trials** had shown that the drugs provided any statistically significant advantage over placebo; this implied a trial failure of 57%. Second, even where the drugs outperformed the placebo, the placebo effects' magnitude was significantly larger than Kirsch and Saperstein had reported in 1998: "**82% of the drug response was duplicated by the placebo response**."[43]

Harrington asserts, "In other words, a mere '18% of the drug response is due to the pharmacological effects of the medication.'

The difference was significant statistically but probably not clinically significant—that is to say, the difference between taking a drug and taking a placebo would probably have not been readily apparent to a patient or his or her doctor outside an experimental trial setting."[44]

Other studies showed similar problems. Psychiatrists Arif Khan and Walter Brown presented data on 19,639 depressed patients in clinical trials that showed no statistically significant difference for suicide risk between those taking active medication and those merely swallowing a placebo each day.[45]

Another unexplained and vexing problem was revealed by **William Potter**, a psychiatrist involved in research for Eli Lilly. He found that both diazepam and Prozac performed very differently in the United States versus Western Europe or South Africa. Much guessing followed, including the suggestion that previous mental health studies had somehow influenced patients and their subsequent responses, but no one knew or has found an answer since. This is despite Potter's pushing a "massive (and semisecret) data-gathering effort called the Placebo Response Drug Trials survey overseen by the Foundation for the National Institutes of Health."[46]

And then another problem, possibly the most fundamental of all, came when researchers examining patient-level data noted that the

---

43 *Harrington, Mind Fixers, 263–4.*

44 *Harrington, Mind Fixers, 264.*

45 *Harrington, Mind Fixers, 264.*

46 *Harrington, Mind Fixers, 265.*

placebo problem was not the only one identified. "Individual patients in the active treatment groups also had profoundly different responses to the drugs. Some responded strongly, others barely at all. It now turned out that all along, there had been a big problem with using rating scales or DSM checklists: two people could be diagnosed with depression—the 'same' disorder—without sharing a single symptom. Small wonder, one might think, that they might not respond to a drug the same way."[47]

In 1997 Merck crowed it was about to "dominate the central nervous system" with its new antidepressant, MK-869, but the drug could not outperform placebos, even though patients reported less hopelessness and anxiety.

The problem was that the placebo, the sugar pill, worked just as well.

In this context of ever-diminishing mental health landmarks and decreasing efficacy, the European Medicines Agency added requirements that parameters defined by an effective biological psychiatry be satisfied. Specifically, outperforming a placebo was no longer the standard; the drug proposed would have to outperform an existing standard of care for drugs already on the market, or predictive biomarkers would have to be demonstrated.[48]

This was a big moment. Harrington quotes a 2010 article saying that Big Pharma had "**run out of brainy ideas**" and was beginning to think about cutting its losses. She notes that "**AstraZeneca, Glaxo Smith Kline, and other big companies have abandoned the field of psychiatry altogether**."[49]

A Recapitulation of Psychiatry's Current Crisis: Let Me Count the Ways.

1. The persistent lack of biological markers of disease precludes addressing the current system of lists of symptoms as valid diseases. Without valid diseases, we simply cannot validly test or validly treat medical entities scientifically.
2. The effectiveness of psychiatry's primary tools to address disease are simply nonexistent in a practical sense. The quantitative

---

47 *Harrington, Mind Fixers, 265.*

48 *Harrington, Mind Fixers, 266.*

49 *Harrington, Mind Fixers, 266.*

assessment of SSRIs and SNRIs reveals that if the effectiveness of the pharmaceutical entity is limited to "**18% of the placebo's effect**," we are simply not treating the disease.

3. And, while not reducing depression, anxiety or PTSD, SSRIs and SNRIs come with lists of obnoxious side effects that include stark personality changes, weight gain and unwanted ventures into diabetes and its complications.
4. Psychiatry is simply not a science guided by statistical definitions and the scientific process.
5. Harrington also mentions other well-recognized problems of psychiatry, including the stigmatizing of mental illness, racial bias and finance-associated inequities of care.
6. And we must not as a society forget psychiatry's greatest misadventure: the millions of schizophrenic patients present in the state hospital system before they were dumped onto our public streets two generations ago. They are still there.
7. But highest on Harrington's list of concerns for psychiatry as currently manifested are two huge elements tied together in a kind of Siamese twin expression of the dark side of capitalism. The **Big Pharma** component of psychiatry is essentially a Willy Loman salesman with a purity of focus on the sale where concern for the quality of the product is nonexistent. *DSM-III* marked biological psychiatry's committed leap into the false hope of overpromise, misleading advertising and billions of dollars in profits with nothing in the way of the effective treatment of mental disease. Her second concern is essentially the flipside of this complaint: "the willingness of so many in recent decades to follow the money instead of the suffering."[50]

Arthur Sackler's Advertising, the Pharmacologic Feedlot and Ketamine

For the first 10 decades of the past 150 years—from approximately 1850 until 1950—we witnessed historically slow progress through profound misunderstandings relating to the working of the mind and the

50 *Harrington, Mind Fixers, 272.*

nature of mental illness and disease. But almost always efforts were sincere and honest, guided by genuine scientific curiosity and human willingness to effect medical aid in situations of disease, pain and suffering. Whether metrazol shock therapy, blaming a perceived schizophrenogenic mother for her child's malady or even Walter Freeman's icepick lobotomies, physician-healers can be seen as wanting to help, as wanting to heal.

In 1998 the Medical Advertising Hall of Fame wrote of **Arthur Sackler** on bestowing him his award for unique contribution, "**No single individual did more to shape the character of medical advertising than the multi-talented Dr. Arthur Sackler of Purdue Pharma fame**. His seminal contribution was bringing the full power of advertising and promotion to pharmaceutical marketing."[51] And it can be argued that advertising was a uniquely effective method to distribute knowledge of newly developed drugs.

But too much money can undo the best of intentions, and soon profits outstripped good judgment and medical efficacy in many situations, leading to untruths being told at great expense, little medical effectiveness and great profits, but much continued suffering by patients treated with nothing more than empty promise. In the depression-anxiety universe, this has led to simple patient predation as enormous numbers of patients are shuffled through varying micro-diagnoses while being kept on a programmed series of worthless medicines. Simple statistics has pointed this out for decades and concern has been expressed, but Big Pharma is simply the big boy on the block and calls many of the shots. The question is where to go when you learn the science you are studying is simply not science, and the medicines you are using to treat disease simply do not work, while the diseases you are treating are not valid entities addressable as disease.

But then, around the year 2000, the general anesthetic **ketamine** was recognized as uniquely effective for the treatment of depression, earning respect in the world's number one science journal, *Nature*, with a February 15, 2018, article from which I will quote the opening sentence: "The discovery of the rapid antidepressant effects of the NMDAR antagonist ketamine is arguably the most important advance in the field of psychiatry in the past half century."[52]

---

51 Podolsky, "Preying on Prescribers," 1785–1787.

52 Yang, "Ketamine blocks bursting in the lateral habenula," 317–322.

In terms of a promise to heal, to heal safely and to also offer genuine accessibility to all during a mental health epidemic, this is an offering to relish beyond all other assertions in psychiatry. Quite simply, ketamine has redefined what is possible with the maladies of depression, anxiety and PTSD.

Elsewhere in this book I discuss the statistics related to my ketamine practice, which is vaguely typical of the response rates boasted by experienced ketamine clinics, all of which are vastly superior to anything claimed by Big Pharma's SSRIs. Even before ketamine, medical professionals and the public alike had been complaining of the extreme overhype of Big Pharma, but now there are numbers to validate their concerns.

Every ketamine clinic knows its effectiveness. Likewise, any Mental Health Industrial Complex knows about ketamine and its threat to its future existence. And, of course, Big Pharma knows this also but is hugely resistant. For the past 20 years we have known of ketamine's antidepressant qualities and the clinics have presented data that cannot be ignored, but Big Pharma has an industry that depends upon the continued flow of SSRIs and SNRIs.

Esketamine, brand name Spravato, is the "lesser half" mirror image of the ketamine molecule as it comes in every bottle of generic ketamine. This portion of the ketamine molecule has demonstrated its antidepressant effectiveness in the FDA's esketamine trials. Its continued suppression cannot be argued as anything but that— suppression.

Whatever the mechanism of containment, the suppression of ketamine is an active process in a passive format that has created a feedlot mentality in the mental health industry, where a vast proportion of the depression-suffering public is being denied the most effective agent ever recognized for the treatment of depression, anxiety and PTSD. This is a huge industry of massive consequence, operating in a decidedly malignant fashion so that Big Pharma may continue to foist personality-changing, diabetes-inducing drugs on a severely ailing populace for enormous profit but minimal effective care.

If we look at the numbers, especially in these Covid-Trumpian times of enormous stress, we see a huge fraction of the American public caught up in this Big Pharma feedlot. This feedlot feeds on a citizenry that includes you and me. It is fed upon by Big Pharma executives in a fashion that may lack the dripping, red blood of a Hollywood film lot showing off its vampires, but let me make clear that the depression left to fester in their supposed patients knows every bit of the pain and suffering portrayed on those silly screens of horror.

And inside of Big Pharma things are going anywhere but better, as I discussed earlier. Most of the big pharmaceuticals have already left and, as psychiatrist David Lieberman makes clear in his own history of psychiatry, *Shrinks*, never has a pharmaceutical drug come to be as a product of intention.[53] Other than the nearly worthless "me too" SSRIs, all major discoveries, such as the tricyclic iproniazid, were discovered by accident or, at most, lucky coincidence. This says that a drug that can claim to be the most significant contribution to psychiatry in the past 50 years is not going away, just as finding a replacement is unlikely; the hope that a similar drug of equal safety will be found soon is minuscule. So far, all the other NMDA blockers studied have not ventured anywhere close to acceptability.

Ketamine is likely here to stay.

Though patients certainly like the idea of an antidepressant that might address their depression, the mental health industry is extremely mixed on the subject. Ketamine practitioners have made their decision, but most other mental health practitioners have affiliations with the Mental Health Industrial Complex with its close ties to Big Pharma, where ketamine is hugely stigmatized, most of the time in a strangely coerced, silly fashion.

If ketamine were to be seen to work and to be safe, practitioners ought to be interested, at the very least. Instead, we see inside of any Mental Health Industrial Complex what we might call the syndrome of **KRPAD**—Ketamine-Related Physician Anxiety and Depression—where practitioners and therapists suffer a specific anxiety and depression that can be attributed to the threat of ketamine eventually replacing most of their mental health tools.

This syndrome's name, KRPAD (pronounced KUR-pad), enjoys its academic debut here.

These KRPAD-suffering practitioners inside the Mental Health Industrial Complex want to do the right thing, of course. But they are, I believe, confused. Many of them need the actual ketamine themselves, but that is just a simple site issue; what these healers want is the best

---

53 Lieberman, Shrinks, 172–182.

and safest tool for their sick patients that they can offer. It happens that in these trying times, ketamine has the most to offer of any drug used to treat depression, anxiety or PTSD. The only comparable agent to ketamine is transcranial magnetic stimulation (TMS). Transcranial magnetic stimulation sounds great, but it is also very high-tech and expensive.

Word has it that TMS also finds enhancement with ketamine, but that is an evolving story for the future.

Any thoughtful summary of the data I have just presented suggests that ketamine should go mainstream. That it is currently "off label" is a product of two decades of monied coercion by Big Pharma to keep ketamine from clearing all the Big Pharma shelves of their SSRIs. To do so Big Pharma has maintained a level of depression and anxiety in its patients, as well as their treating physicians and other caregivers, that is unconscionably enormous. Numbers here for the United States are in the 30–60 million category, while for the rest of the planet they are correspondingly larger.

Now, Big Pharma will never budge without a huge push from money. To me, that says that Big Pharma will never release ketamine as an "on label" product. Big Pharma would have to pay for the studies that would free ketamine to destroy its industry. It will not happen, certainly not while most Mental Health Industrial Complex therapists and practitioners harbor KRPAD-related fears of ketamine.

Before moving on to "The Instructive Case of Dr. C.," I want to make one last point that ought to make the use of ketamine for depression appealing to psychiatry, especially all those wanna-be biological psychiatrists with science on their mind. The *Nature* article describing the **lateral habenula (LHb)** as our brain organ of despair is beautiful on many levels. Its description of the LHbM is exquisite. All this beauty aside, if the LHbM does not qualify as a biologic marker, then it could be argued with equally absurd invalidity that Sigmund Freud did not singlehandedly fetishize cigars even as he smoked them. There is big and disruptive science here, unless the article is invalid, but this is an article from the most respected scientific journal in the world, *Nature*. At the very least, Western scientists have the obligation—which they should soon acknowledge—to either validate the LHbM or challenge it.

At this moment in time, the LHbM is a biologic marker seen in mice but not yet recognized in humans. The habenular nuclei and their activities are, however, much preserved among the vertebrates, especially in the ventral habenula (VHb). The LHb is a relatively flexible entity and will probably demonstrate changes in function that reflect the unparalleled evolution of the human brain, the human psyche and the creature of society that is us.[54] But possibly the greatest moral crime coming from the suppression of ketamine would not be the simple, default forcing of a maintenance of depression upon a patient who would prefer to be cured by his psychiatrist but, rather, the complete shutdown of research relating to ketamine.

After all, an entire planet ridden by depression, anxiety and PTSD quivers in hopeful anticipation of a product that is here but cannot be accessed by the vast majority of the citizenry because of the bullying SSRIs, SNRIs and psychiatrists standing in the way of their mental normalcy and happiness. I have yet to meet a psychiatrist who has read this article, though I have mentioned it to dozens. Does that mean something? The article is from China. Does that mean something? If the LHb is truly a brain organ of despair, research psychiatrists have something to study. And if they do, has biologic psychiatry been born? Very, very possibly.

The Instructive Case of Dr. C.

Early in my career, back in the 1980s while working as an emergency medicine physician, I spent several years in a community hospital in Southern California. It became immediately obvious that one of the older physicians, Dr. C., had suffered some event compromising mentation. A number of his medical errors were discussed in hospital hallways, but no one seemed to know what to do about the dangerous doctor as patients continued to suffer.

The situation was new to me, but it was obvious that a change was necessary. The problems continued for a week or so until finally the local hospital authorities took it upon themselves to remove the doctor from his practice. The exact mechanisms utilized then I was not privy to, and I do not know the mechanisms that would be utilized now, but I do know that reporting a disabled physician is now a routine event. There is, in short, a mechanism to deal with disabled physicians.

---

54 *Isaac H. Blanco and Stephen W Wilson, "The habenular nuclei: a conserved asymmetric relay station in the vertebrate brain," Philosophical Transactions of the Royal Society, 364 (4 December 2008): 105–106.*

So, what do we do in this situation where we are so obviously denying ketamine, an elixir of a particular health of sorts, to our very needy patients? We know that agents of Big Pharma, like commissars of Leninist Russia, are stationed at key positions in every academic and medical institution for the purposes of maintaining the current SSRI status quo. Big Pharma is not going to move over and suddenly allow us to stop abusing our patients and, as mental health practitioners, we are hugely reluctant to even begin to admit that we share responsibility.

We need guidance.

I suggest that we look to Dr. C to help us recognize dysfunction when we need to, do what it takes to get ketamine on label as it most certainly should be, and ensure that this single greatest contribution to psychiatry in the last half century is utilized with the respect, compassion and simple utilitarian effectiveness that this magnificent, happiness-availing blessing has to offer our Covid and Trump-troubled society.

America will be a better place for it.

But how do we do this? So far, they have not listened to me. Very much the opposite, in fact. For the past 3 years, I have been dealing with the local medical licensure officials who have spent 3 years trying to learn the subtleties of anesthesia as presented by the university's only partially committed ketamine clinic, which presents itself superficially as being in direct competition with my own clinic. As I am about to discuss, however, it is coming from a quite different place.

My clinic is one of the busiest ketamine providers in the country. We have seen more than 3,000 patients and administered over 11,000 treatments with no major medical problems suffered. Prior to the entrance of esketamine (Spravato) to the market, this agency wanted to remove my medical license based on its off-label usage and the questionable "anesthesia" being performed. This directive came primarily from the local university's ketamine clinic who one would be forgiven for thinking was acting from its own specific competitive interests.

The university clinic is indeed in competition with my own, but it is not a situation of ketamine competing with ketamine; the university clinic, I would assert, participates in a bait and switch operation capitalizing on the public conversations about ketamine, but then consistently underdosing the individual ketamine treatments at the same time it is deliberately screening patients away from the more effective ketamine procedure. I interpret the clinic's behavior to suggest it has found a sweet spot where ketamine's fame pulls patients into its Mental Health Industrial Complex meat grinder, where they are then redirected to other more remunerative procedures such as TMS or ECT. Whatever their incentive, we are adequately treating their patients who must then suffer the mediocre results of their mediocre products.

In any case, after Spravato's demonstration of efficacy in dealing with depression, that quest to take my license was partially dropped, but I hold it up as an example of typical behavior of an SSRI-dependent mental health structure under siege by the reality of the supremely efficacious threat of ketamine. Patients need ketamine—it is the only medicine that works for depression. TMS also works, but it does so even better with ketamine, rumors suggest.

Psychiatrists and therapists in their high towers eventually find themselves resistant to their usual tools and need ketamine. I see a few university practitioners who, to the public, disguise themselves in casual clothes, change their names and come in for stealth ketamine treatments. The KRPAD syndrome fits a few of them, but most are simply suffering the depression, anxiety and PTSD that currently afflicts every society on the planet.

Big Pharaoh Pharma

If the term "people" excluded only those associated with Big Pharma and referred to practitioners and therapists as well as the usual mental health patients, then we would have at least one option to direct at the ketamine-eschewing Mental Health Industrial Complex. Perhaps if I were Moses fresh from whacking a tribe of SSRI-imbibing Midianites, I could turn toward the Pharaoh who was busy directing an entourage scurrying about beneath gilded canopies fluttering beside a freshly painted sphinx and wail, "Let my people go!"

The pharaoh never listened, says scripture, and neither will Big Pharma as long as the money flows, but eventually the insurance companies should find guidance in their better angels of capitalism. And if Big Pharaoh Pharma eventually embraces the most significant contribution to psychiatry of the past half century, and learns to administer ketamine to an entire society, that society will know a level of total joy and communal prosperity that it has never previously known or even considered.

After all, there has never been a people able to address stress, depression and PTSD as we are doing today with ketamine. We could be the first genuinely happy society—top to bottom—on the planet since Gobekli Tepe (the only society with monumental architecture but no police or bureaucracy). Maybe even happier.

And what of the science of ketamine? Psychiatry says it wants science in its description but gets distracted by the billions. Surely some

Western scientists are ready to define the LHBM. To explore the LHb and its most mysterious burst mode is to define at least this part of mental health as providing an actual biologic marker that at the same time gives psychiatry strutting rights as a true, genuinely scientific entity.

With ketamine, biologic psychiatry has finally and truly found a genuine place for itself in the honored hallways of science.

CHAPTER 3

Shooting Elephants

In Chapter 2 we watched psychiatry's mojo wane in lockstep to revelations about the universal shortcomings of its antidepressants—they just do not work—as well as the fundamental failure of the **DSM** system to define diseases by lists of symptoms. I also made the point that **ketamine** has a unique efficacy that relieves depression profoundly with great safety in a high percentage of people, that psychiatry knows and understands ketamine's profound utility but—despite that knowledge—psychiatry refuses to involve itself with ketamine. Psychiatry will not even discuss ketamine.

In fact, the dirty little fact of the matter is that it is doing everything it can to suppress ketamine.

But as repeated multiple times in this book, the science journal *Nature* asserted ketamine's status as a shunned but uniquely valuable offering to psychiatry.[55] And by every measure both academic and anecdotal—during these times of Donald Trump, Covid–19 and Facebook predation—depression, anxiety and PTSD have been increasing in every category.

Current figures for depression, anxiety and PTSD are especially dynamic during Covid's pandemic sway. Recognizing this imprecision and its volatility, I find the figures that I presented earlier in the chapter on scientific nomenclature ballpark acceptable: 50–60 million Americans—almost one-sixth of the population—have been touched by the stress diseases and would likely benefit much from treatment with ketamine.

If ketamine enjoys a **75% response rate** where SSRIs know only the response rate of "**18% of a placebo**," which, per the investigator, "would not be detectable by the patient or the investigator outside of a trial

55 *Yang, "Ketamine blocks bursting in the lateral habenula," 317–322.*

setting" why, we all ask, isn't academic psychiatry utilizing ketamine?[56] These figures amount to a ketamine/SSRI efficacy ratio of 30–40 times; ketamine is at least **30–35 times more effective** than SSRIs when treating depression, anxiety or PTSD.

What? Ketamine is 30–35 times more effective? And psychiatry will not discuss ketamine as an antidepressant? But **Spravato** is ketamine, isn't it? Yes, for all genuinely practical purposes, it is.

I cannot speak for every, or even for most, high-tower medical establishments across the country, but in Utah ketamine for depression functions much as a rogue agent. (Spravato is ketamine made financially acceptable to the other pharmaceutical establishments by increasing its price to noncompetitive—and therefore non-frightening—levels.) Of the two local institutions in Utah, one, Intermountain Healthcare, does not to my knowledge provide ketamine in its generic form, and the other, the **University of Utah**, operates what I would call a "**failed- treatment depression clinic**" where SSRI failures are given token ketamine as a means of getting them into the system rather than treating them with a fully effective ketamine process, meaning the higher doses required for longer depression-free intervals.

Additionally, while ketamine clinics are popping up, establishment high-tower medical systems fear ketamine's threat to their SSRIs and support the aggressive control of ketamine clinics through local, extra-constitutional systems of administrative law known for their commonplace trampling on the rights of individual physicians.

What is going on here? America is based on systems of law, but this Utah Division of Occupational and Professional Licensing (**DOPL**) entity is simply not the stuff of law as we have come to know it from either the US Constitution or our personal sense of what is right and what is wrong. And yet DOPL officials are generally at least reasonably honorable men not intending to break laws or do despicable things. But when a higher authority identifies an entity as dangerous, they demonstrate that they are willing to soil themselves with untruth and otherwise undeserved malice.

But it is the **higher authority**, I would assert, that carries the burden of responsibility.

The problem is that our distance from the events precludes

---

56 *Harrington, Mind Fixers, 262–266.*

our understanding them, especially when the agents of the events constantly shape them to their own advantage. Nothing new here; we all understand the issue of fake news after four recent years of political focus on it, but with an entity of the size, sophistication, financial power and intellectual self-absorption of **Big Pharma** and academic psychiatry, there can be consequences, especially if deception plays any initial role. I contend that deception does play a key role and that George Orwell's definition and criticism of the British Raj in particular and the British empire in general can help us understand **Big Pharma** and its influence on both academic and practical psychiatry. For, make no mistake, Big Pharma and academic psychiatry constitute an entity that fulfills the definition of empire as thoroughly as the promise of teatime structures an Englishman's afternoon.

As Eric Blair, **Orwell's** given name, he served the **British Raj** during the 1920s as a subdivisional police officer where, he says, "In a job like that you get to see the dirty work of empire at close quarters."[57] He was young and describes himself as "ill-educated," able to "get nothing in perspective" and personally oppressed with "an intolerable sense of guilt" at "the scarred buttocks of the men who had been flogged with bamboos."

In a 1936 essay entitled "**Shooting an Elephant**," he describes all Indian society as oppressed and resentful, but their response was uneven.

> "The young Buddhist priests were the worst of all. [They] seemed to have nothing to do but stand on street corners and jeer at Europeans... I did not even know that the British Empire is dying, still less did I know that it is a great deal better than the younger empires that are going to supplant it. All I knew was that I was stuck between my hatred of the Empire I served and my rage against the evil-spirited little beasts who tried to make my job impossible. With one part of my mind I thought of the British Raj as an unbreakable tyranny, as something clamped down, in *saecula saeculorum*, upon the will of prostrate peoples; with another part I thought that the greatest joy in the world would be to drive a bayonet into a Buddhist priest's guts. Feelings like these are the

57 Har- court Publishing, 1981): 148–155.

> normal by-products of imperialism; ask any Anglo–Indian official, if you can catch him off duty."[58]

As a Raj official, Mr. Blair was once called upon to deal with a mad elephant, an apparently commonplace thing that he describes as insignificant, but it turned out to be an event that gave him "a better glimpse than I had had before of the real nature of imperialism—the real motives for which despotic governments act."

The elephant had gone "**must**," a routine, periodic, though potentially dangerous rage that domestic elephants suffer, but that can usually be easily managed by the elephant's "mahout" or manager. Unfortunately, the mahout had gone the wrong direction in looking for the crazy elephant and was now ten miles away. In following the elephant, Blair acquired a crowd of 2,000 onlookers and an elephant

George Orwell, A Collection of Essays, (New York: Houghton Mifflin gun to deal with the unexpected. He makes clear he had no intention of actually using the gun or killing the elephant, and when he finally came upon the offending beast it was peacefully eating grass, confirming his hopes for a peaceful outcome. But it was not to be.

> "Suddenly I realized that I should have to shoot the elephant after all. The people expected it of me, and I had got to do it; I could feel their 2000 wills pressing me forward irresistibly. And it was at this moment, as I stood there with the rifle in my hands, that I first grasped the hollowness, the futility of the white man's dominion in the East ... I perceived in this moment that when the white man turns tyrant it is his own freedom that he destroys. He becomes a sort of hollow, opposing dummy, the conventionalized figure of a Sahib. For it is the condition of his rule that he shall spend his life in trying to impress the 'natives,' and so in every crisis he has got to do what the 'natives' expected of him. He wears a mask, and his face grows to fit it. I had to shoot the elephant."[59]

58 *Orwell, Collection of Essays, 148–155.*

59 *Orwell, Collection of Essays, 148–155.*

This incident gives us a peek at the fundamental hypocrisy required of an official of the British Empire, but to make the case that a political-economic entity like Big Pharma shares much of the basic structure, motivation and dysfunction of the British Empire we must go to another essay in this George Orwell collection, entitled "Rudyard Kipling."

Orwell describes Kipling as boyishly naive.

> "He could not understand what was happening, because he had never had any grasp of the economic forces underlying imperial expansion. It is notable that Kipling does not seem to realize, any more than the average soldier or colonial administrator, that an empire is primarily a moneymaking concern. Imperialism as Kipling sees it is a sort of forcible evangelizing. You turn a Gatling gun on a mob of unarmed 'natives,' and then you establish 'the Law,' which includes roads, railways and a courthouse.

"We all live by robbing Asiatic coolies, and those of us who are 'enlightened' all maintain that those coolies ought to be set free; but our standard of living, and hence our 'enlightenment,' demands that the robbery shall continue."[60]

So, we have a portrait of the **British Empire** from **Orwell** that asserts a fundamental corruption that arises from the very nature of the relationship between the British Raj and the subjugated peoples of the India it ruled. Does **Big Pharma** share attributes of the British Raj that, if recognized and addressed, could lead to significant improvements in the delivery of mental health care to the citizens of America?

How, then, is Big Pharma like the British Raj? First, the essential nature of their being—the corporation—defines their motivations, their primary concerns, their leadership structure, their public image, the tools of power available to them, the public and private values and their differences that are in constant dynamic competition as well as the lies that must be told to maintain that bottom line.

A corporation is a created, nonmaterial entity legally structured as an individual citizen while addressing a particular economic function as it protects its members from liability. Incorporation is a means to constrain the risk of risky projects to the risky projects only, while protecting other

---

60 *Orwell, Collection of Essays, 116–131.*

projects. The range of corporate enterprise is huge. At one extreme, the limited liability corporation or LLC, the entrepreneur is looking for tax advantages and liability protections, and probably saves a few dollars over the course of the life of the business.

At the other extreme might be the **East India Company**, or **EIC**, a corporation whose right to exist the queen granted to Robert Clive in 1600. The EIC was inspired by chests of jewels and gold and the Far Eastern spices Sir Francis Drake brought back in the hold of his ship, the *Golden Hind*, and whose initial directive was to break Spain and Portugal's spice trade monopoly. The EIC was also chartered to trade in cotton, silk, indigo, tea and slaves.

The company was successful, and its charter expanded to include conquering a subcontinent, submitting those peoples to its rule, restructuring the many local economies to enhance that of Britain and then to plunder that wealth. East India Company success on military, cultural and economic fronts eventually led to intervention by the British government and the establishment of the **British Raj** in 1858—that is, direct rule by the British government rather than the intermediary of the **EIC**. Local estimates of British wealth extraction over the course of two centuries reach **$300 trillion**.

Somewhere between these two extremes of a local LLC and the British Raj lies the collection of independent corporations that together constitute the Medical Industrial Complex that is **Big Pharma**. Big Pharma will be revealed to have participated in several untoward activities—which we justly criticize—but it started no wars, conquered no peoples, overtly killed no one, delivered no corporal punishment, deindustrialized no culture and forcibly evangelized no one.

But being the corporations that they are, money is their shared, primary concern and, as such, leads to decisions that might not be agreeable to human, biologic systems—that is, to people—simply because they do not enjoy the same priority as that bottom line. It is not that they do not empathize with their fellow human beings; it is simply that money has priority, and its bottom-line consideration must always preempt other, lesser values, such as human well-being.

Times have changed since Robert Clive won the EIC charter in 1600. Four hundred and twenty years ago violence was an omnipresent, casual affair where a disagreement at lunch might end in a dispute being settled with the sword at one's side and the death of a dinner companion. **Orwell** termed the men who focused on the subcontinent "Anglo-Indians" and described them as incomparable men of action that got things done and "changed the face of the earth."[61]

Times have indeed changed, but the soul of a corporation has not, and there will always be men seeking to utilize their powers to maximum advantage. Nations and the societies within them have dealt with many varieties of this power struggle since the first formal corporations of Rome. The **EIC** eventually became so big and powerful that England took it over, evolving the company into the military–political entity known as the **British Raj**, which lasted until the peaceful struggles of **Mahatma Gandhi** and partition in 1948.

Where today can we find the soul of these men in the modern **Big Pharma**? Their daily violence in the form of the virtual master–slave relationships tuned with the bamboo flog, casual war, a thousand varieties of disguised theft and the constant indignities of rigid class systems are gone. But if we google "**Big Pharma dysfunction**" we come up with a list of issues in a 2018 article by Katie Dwyer entitled "6 Critical Risks Facing the Pharmaceutical Industry"[62] that reveal a great, bulky, tyrant-sort-of-thing that constantly resists laws and conventions to its own economic advantage.

1. **Generic drug competition**. Expiration of a patent should allow access by duplicate generic drugs from other manufacturers. But, where two competitors lower the price by 52% and nine competitors by 30% more, pharmaceuticals that resist guidelines illegally make money, adding much to drug prices. Every time-related stall makes more money. Pharmaceuticals have even learned from the chef who always leaves out a key ingredient; inaccurate drug recipes forestall competitors gaining market share. All of this is the product of technically illegal sway that derives from the bottom-line superseding ethics of the pharmaceutical industry.
2. **Opioid addiction liability**. The **Sackler family** and Purdue Pharmaceutical foisted a patient-hostile, corner- drug-pusher level of morality on the public and is resultantly dealing with an addiction problem of its own manufacture as it faces many

---

61 *Orwell, Collection of Essays, 148–155.*

62 *Katie Dwyer, "6 Critical Risks Facing the Pharmaceutical Industry," (June 29, 2018): (http://riskandinsurance.com/author/katie-dwyer).*

levels of federal and state prosecution for the original FDA opiate illegalities. This feasting is very much in the mode of **Orwell's** Anglo-Indian predators and is remarkably similar to Britain's opiate wars with China, except that here in America the predatory entity is feeding on its own citizens. The British were at least racists and extreme snobs of culture who believed the "coolie culture" they were exploiting was genuinely inferior; that presumed racial difference pronounced the whole colonial abomination somewhat less of a crime.

Few in our times believe publicly in such racist, autocratic bigotry. What, then, are we to say of the people of **Big Pharma** defrauding their own neighbors of wealth and happiness? There is a big difference here, and it's important, not so much in the crime perpetrated or the people abused, but in the minds of the abusers; feeding on your own seems fundamentally worse than feeding on more distant peoples, perhaps in the same mode as Stephen King's assertion in the book *The Shining* that the ultimate biologic crime is to murder one's own kin. I return to this topic of feedlot mentality when discussing the suppression of **ketamine**.

3. **Product liability**. Development of a pharmaceutical implies risk. On many levels this subject is being discussed. Many times, the issue is one of safety versus money. Integrity is an important parameter and is specifically questionable in an entity like a pharmaceutical with its demonstrable devotion to the bottom line at the expense of human safety. Trust but verify, a phrase from nuclear negotiations, is applicable here.
4. Keeping up with technology is apparently an issue. A pharmaceutical's enormous size confers a special influence that somehow allows this to be less of a concern.
5. **Counterfeit drugs and global quality control**. As overseas drug manufacture increases, this gets to be a significant problem. This issue lends itself to our concern with corporate attitude; swashbuckling drug deals can take place here and might even rival the British Raj–China opium trade where "the opium shipped to China accounted for 40% of the Raj's revenue."
6. **Patent cliffs**. When a drug reaches the end of its patent, sales drop markedly. As a product of multiple mechanisms, $50

billion in prescription drugs is at stake. This issue flows into that of generic drug competition where **Big Pharma** has many unsavory and anticompetitive options.

This list paints a portrait of the sway of the pharmaceutically powerful and, I think, effectively implies legal, human and psychological connections to those swashbuckling Anglo-Indians of the **EIC**. If those same buccaneers were born today into a situation where they might end up as CEOs in a pharmaceutical, I believe their conduct would differ little from the hungry manner that pharmaceutical CEOs demonstrate daily.

Focusing on **ketamine**, the following is an evidentiary list of the ongoing dysfunction of Big Pharma and the adherents—both willing and unwilling—to its ongoing, self-serving, citizenry-denying protection of its **SSRIs** by the suppression of **ketamine**, "the most significant contribution to psychiatry in the past half century." I discuss each entity.

1. **Ketamine suppression** for the past 20 years.
2. Suppression of the *Nature* article that reveals the biological origins of neurologic depression, as well as ketamine's ability to abate the specific process related to the psychological entity that is depression.
3. **KRPAD—Ketamine-Related Physician Anxiety and Depression**, a mental disorder of practitioners not allowed to use effective antidepressants, either for their patients or for themselves.
4. **Dr. Faust and DOPL**: an example of yesterday's swashbuckler, fraudulent, dollar-devoted, patient- damaging attitude from a modern, high-tower academic Mental Health Industrial Complex.
5. **DOPL**, Utah's **Department of Professional Licensing**, a naïve, generally honorable-of-intention agency that lends itself to the wishes of **Big Pharma** by way of the bottom- line corporate directives of Dr. Faust and his associates.

Ketamine Suppression

Big Pharma has known for the past 20 years that **ketamine** is effective in treating depression. That ketamine is effective was formally validated with the FDA approval of **Spravato**, essentially ketamine under a shabby cloaking device meant to keep reasonably priced ketamine from the public. This, I assert, is an example of manipulative, bottom-line, fundamentally not-of-the-rules suppression of ketamine at the expense of the populace.

The unforeseen consequence of this maneuver is to reveal that ketamine works, despite the subterfuge. The frightening and disheartening part of this is that we know that every academic institution in America knows the true value of ketamine, but they still suppress it. Of course, this COULD mean that they are all consistent in their evaluation of ketamine—and that ketamine is somehow too difficult to deliver to patients—but I do not see that as likely. In their successful treatment of depression, every ketamine clinic in America is testimony to ketamine's safe and easy access to the public, and it will only get easier with growing experience.

The most disheartening component of this situation is that for the common decision regarding the suppression of **ketamine** to have taken place, it must have been discussed throughout the world of academic psychiatry. This what-to-do-with-ketamine topic has to have been echoing down the hallways of every university and high-tower **Mental Health Industrial Complex** in the country. And in every one of those CEOs' offices, they came to the same corrupt conclusion. How could such a complicated consistency in the presentation of known falsehoods not be a product of collusion?

That dark word. Our professors, at least some of them must, then, be racketeers of a sort. Are there **RICO** violations of the highest order ongoing in virtually every high-tower and academic medical institution in America? Big tobacco and Facebook are the models to utilize in the measure of whatever justice is being compromised.

Additionally, and somewhat of this theme, was a recent **ACLU** case that defined the jailing of opiate-addicted personnel who went on to suffer withdrawal without treatment as human rights violations. If this is so, isn't denial of **ketamine**—a product recognized to be uniquely effective in the treatment of depression—and subsequent default treatment with worthless **SSRIs** or **SNRIs**, a denial of our right to happiness—or at least the pursuit of happiness—a constitutionally guaranteed proposition? From the above-mentioned article, I believe it is. I am beginning conversation with the ACLU on this topic.[63]

---

63 *Ingrid Binswanger, "Opioid Use Disorder and Incarceration – Hope for Ensuring the Continuity of Treatment," New England Journal of Medicine 380:13 (March 28, 2019): 1193–1195.*

You know them by their lack of ketamine and their fine, three-piece suits. May the depositions begin.

Suppression of the Nature Article

You know them also by their lack of education. It is my belief that the foundational article defining biologic depression in humans is the February 15, 2018, *Nature* entry entitled "**Ketamine Blocks Bursting in the Lateral Habenula to Rapidly Relieve Depression**" by Yan Yang and colleagues. But I have yet to meet a psychiatrist, psychologist or any other practitioner who has read this article.[64]

Depression, most of the time, is simply not an error of physiology; It is an evolutionary, selected-for, medically defensive response meant to deal with a threatening situation involving thwarted ambition. But there are exceptions. Physiology does contribute a chemical imbalance that alters a mental state. Hypoglycemia and hyponatremia satisfy that definition, but they do not produce depression as we mean the word; I would think that we will find evidence for affliction sources of depression, but they will be relatively limited.

Usually, depression involves choice.

Andrew Solomon in his reflective tome, *The Noonday Demon*, begins an insightful argument that asserts that thwarted ambition operates at intimate intensity to produce depression, which is itself at least in part a thing of choice.[65] We observe the world around us, make evaluations and then choose. If the world is sufficiently unyielding and "thwarts ambition," induces despair or simply presents unrelenting pain, depression can become an option of choice.

Why haven't the psychiatrists read this article? Why haven't they yet substituted "**thwarted ambition**" for "chemical imbalance?" Though I have no evidence, other than the consistent suppression of any mention of **ketamine** in academic circles, I believe it was the article's opening sentence that determined its doom in Western medicine. In that first defining sentence, the antidepressant effects of ketamine are lauded as "**the most important advance in psychiatry in the past half century**."

Combined with the general suppression of ketamine as mentioned

---

64 *Yang, "Ketamine blocks bursting in the lateral habenula," 317–322.*

65 *Andrew Solomon, The Noonday Demon, (New York: Simon & Shuster, May 2015).*

in the previous section, the suppression of this article is monumental. Besides simply pointing to ketamine as an effective agent, the article describes the intimate biology of the **LHb**, the physiology of the NMDA receptor and the unparalleled recognition and discovery of the **LHBM** that defines a programmed, neurologic mechanism for the induction and presence of depression.

Any psychiatrist, psychologist or therapist on any level who is not aware of this article is academically deficient, but I am quite sure it is not entirely their fault. Just how **Big Pharma** goes about influencing therapists at the practitioner level to suppress academic articles of this importance, I have no idea. But that they have done it, I have little doubt, and academic psychiatry's consistent ignorance of this article is testimony to that dark influence.

KRPAD: Ketamine-Related Physician Anxiety and Depression

As I mentioned earlier, mental health practitioners who must administer anything but **ketamine**, know both that they are denying their patients effective treatment, and that ketamine's growing popularity will eventually replace the pharmaceuticals upon which they now depend. Who wouldn't be anxious and depressed at this triple whammy of not being able to care for your patients, knowing that a superior product was soon to come that would threaten your livelihood and understanding that the anxiety and depression that you are suffering will not be relieved by your own medicines?

The only thing that will relieve these people is the very medicine that they are at this very moment denying to their own patients. Though there is some clumsy justice here, patients are still being condemned by this feedlot capitalism to suffering the worst disease known to humankind, depression. May the tens of thousands of therapists suffering this malady speak up.

As I asserted in the previous chapter, "**Let my people go!**"

Dr. Faust and DOPL

Dr. Faust (defined as any of several university physicians actively sharing anti-ketamine sentiments) participates in the treatment-resistant depression clinic at the local university. He was also intimately involved with Utah's **Department of Professional Licensing (DOPL)** in discussing with the investigator whether my clinic was in violation of various parameters of treatment.

I believe him (or her) to be as aggressive and inappropriately hostile in their assertions about my clinic as they are in fundamental violation of their Hippocratic oaths. They are doing their patients even more wrong than they are me.

Dr. Faust became involved in my DOPL case directly by becoming an expert witness, despite his obvious economic conflicts. Whether Dr. Faust became involved with my clinic under the general theme of **Big Pharma's suppression of ketamine**, or whether he is an economic competitor striving to reduce competition, I cannot know. But the information I have gleaned from our interaction gives much insight into his motivation for giving ketamine.

The local university clinic advertises for the **ketamine** treatment of depression but, per Dr. Faust's expert witness testimony, **30% of those patients are immediately diverted elsewhere**. Dr. Faust then gives only a minimal dose of ketamine; his minimalist results are a damning testimony to that deficiency.

The clinic gets exactly the results expected if the ketamine dose is limited to **0.5 mg per kilogram IV over 40 minutes**, which is the standard ketamine dose described by Dr. Sanacora for the minimal elicitation of a psychedelic experience, an entirely different medical objective than the therapeutic one newly ascribed to Dr. Faust's ketamine.

The clinic advertises what I would describe as the worst ketamine for depression results that I have seen published in the industry.

I regard Dr. Faust not as an assailant who is really after me, but rather as one of the players in that situation of the **Raj** described by **Orwell** where he is caught in a bind. I am almost certain that he appreciates the potential of ketamine. I am also almost certain that he would not be allowed to give higher, more effective doses by his university superiors. I even doubt his own initiative at directing **DOPL** in its aggressiveness. But, short of a deposition, I will probably never know his genuine motivation. But it is all of one piece; the consistency gives us the truth.

Corporate money has the priority—and with that valuing—patient well-being necessarily takes a back seat.

So, where does Dr. Faust fit in the Orwell short story "**Shooting an Elephant**"? I would hope he is frustrated at not being able to deliver adequate care, and I would hope he resents doing the things he had to do for money. If so, I would hope he would suffer the same feelings Orwell knew when forced into the role of the reluctant imperialist. Though I am not at all certain into exactly whose abdomen he should be lusting to place the bayonet, basic human honor ought to require that a choice has been made.

I hope to one day put that most penetrating of questions regarding varieties of abdominal preference to Dr. Faust.

DOPL, Utah's Department of Professional Licensing

These men, though the focus of everything, are just doing their job, a job that depends for its accuracy on the judgments of others. They have suggested wrongdoing but have not been able to demonstrate it. In their primary area of concern—the **anesthesia** produced by **ketamine**—understanding for them is difficult. They are lawyers or ex-policemen—not medical personnel—and these are quite sophisticated medical questions. When understanding comes from motives that depart significantly from scientific truth, dysfunction is much more commonly the expected result.

From my clinic, among the busiest in the country, I am about to publish a ketamine study demonstrating that my stepped ketamine process for treating depression, **KISSD**, is one of the most effective pharmacologic treatments for depression available anyplace on the planet. At the local university, then, we have the least effective ketamine treatment in the country living next door to the most effective ketamine treatment, and then trying to take it out of business. That, dear reader, is corporate thinking of the thinnest **EIC** variety, minus the swords, the swashbuckling and the thoughts of nobility, of course.

So, here I sit, waiting for state agencies to decide on their level of **Big Pharma** adherence. Am I to be the **elephant** to **Dr. Faust's** subdivisional police officer with a gun? Is his **DOPL**-directed bullet speeding toward my brain, a brain I am proud to say holds the dream of curing ten million American minds of the worst disease known to humankind?

Dr. Faust, please, "**let my people go!**"

CHAPTER 4

What, Exactly, Is Depression?

A part of depression's function is to serve as a signal to one's associates that things have changed in the life of the depressed, and that future relationships with this depressed person will therefore be different. We all recognize the emotion of sadness that characterizes depression, but the sources of depression are hugely complex, ancient, mostly undefined and mostly unrecognized, as are the many varieties of depression syndromes that can result. Genetics, environment and some level of personal choice combine with nearly infinite complexity and subtlety to produce a disease that may lay claim to a role of practical and evolutionary importance that makes the entity of depression far more than just a disease. It is, rather, a psycho- evolutionary option that plays out in our individual daily lives as it also plays out on history on a larger scale to influence our evolution and future as an apex species on this planet.

At a recent ketamine-for-depression conference, one of the speakers spent two hours giving the audience a list of neurochemical, neurotransmitter and other biochemical pathways that could influence behavior and mood in negative ways to produce depression. These mechanisms were presented as somewhat random and accidental, such as catching the wrong virus or ingesting Flint, Michigan lead. They were all valid possibilities—but they were also deemed accidental—accidental where the real world on this point is filled with intention, however inscrutable that intention might be. I term this simplest mode of acquiring mental illness the "**affliction**" mechanism of depression, and place within it the much-embraced chemical imbalance theory manufactured by the manufacturers of SSRIs and SNRIs.

But depression is demonstrably composed of of so much more than simple, almost accidental, negative events. It is, rather, a psycho-evolutionary tool whose origins and consequences are only just beginning to be understood. The story is turning out to be far more complex and filled with intention and big-picture normalcy than we had ever imagined.

I present here four academic papers that give some insight into this new thinking on the development and ultimate workings of brain and mind. In discussing them, I examine the origins and nature of depression as products of four distinct categories of mechanism:

1. **Affliction**. Depression could be random sand in the cogs of the machine that is the brain that produces the ultimate example of what we term an abstraction, the abstraction- producing entity of mind itself. This theory says that a chemical imbalance here, an extra gene copy there, produces the disease in question. That this general mechanism plays a role is almost certain in limited circumstances, but that it is the primary, stand-alone mechanism of depression is almost certainly wrong, as evidenced by the papers and arguments to follow.
2. **Genetic proclivity**. Schizophrenia, autism, bipolar disease and major depression all have genetic predispositions; they are all diseases whose likelihoods are statistically increased when family members share the same disease. But these diseases are not simply inherited. Other major factors consign the genetics to relatively minor influences.
3. **Choice**. We choose our joys when available, and we choose to avoid pain and discomfort when we can. Many joys manifest as dreams beyond attainment owing to the unique circumstances of someone's life; it has been said that there are only "**four jobs worth having: movie star, rock star, sports star, and president**." Holding such a belief, as do so many of our over-digitalized teens, might very well lead to a "**hierarchy conflict**" (one of multiple possibilities explained in the evolutionary psychiatry paper in the coming pages) capable of pushing a mind to choose the neuronal system of a predefined set of behaviors and mood states that characterize the social withdrawal and negative emotions that in turn characterize the entities of mood defined as depression. That this mental movement is a product of choice rather than simple affliction is a statement testifying to depression's role as a valuable option utilized many times over

the course of evolution by humankind and the wide variety of cultures that we have created along the way.

4. **Neurodevelopmental psychiatric disease**. Schizophrenia, autism and bipolar disease are all products of the immune system's developmental and behavioral influences on the central nervous system, specifically altered **dendritic pruning**. With schizophrenia, the key event is a viral infection that overstimulates CD4 immune cells to prune more dendrites than would normally be the case during the routine event of adolescent dendritic pruning. Autism and bipolar disease—also diseases related to dendritic pruning—owe much of their difference in disease to the timing of the initial viral infection and the type of immune response effecting the changes. Though major depressive disorder (**MDD**) and **attention deficit hyperactivity disorder (ADHD)** are recognized to be underpinned by immuno-inflammatory processes, no specific ties to the major histocompatibility complex/ human leukocyte antigen (**MHC/HLA**) system have been recognized for these entities as they have for schizophrenia, autism and bipolar disease, but the authors are still looking and say that they expect to find connections. They believe connections are likely, but the lack of evidence "may reflect the extreme heterogeneity of psychiatric disorders in a highly polygenic context where the MHC/HLA contribution may thus be difficult to unmask."[66]

The purpose of this chapter is not to provide critical facts necessary for the treatment of depression in a practical, mechanistic sense. In fact, I would argue that the primary function of this chapter is to follow and underline multiple times Anne Harrington's directive from her most excellent book *The Mind Fixers*, in which she first notes psychiatry's fundamental lack of science and effective medicine; she then promotes humility. Major humility, I would assert.[67]

These four studies suggest a profound variety of depression entities

---

66 *Ryad Tamouza, Rajagopal Krishnamoorthy, and Marion Leboyer, "Understanding the genetic contribution of the human leukocyte antigen system to common major psychiatric disorders in a world pandemic context," Brain, Behavior, and Immunity Vol 91 (05 October 2020): 731–739.*

67 *Harrington, Mind Fixers, 271–276.*

massively influenced by our immune systems and choice. As has happened so often in the history of psychiatry and the quest to understand the unfathomable brain, the ultimate real-world answers to our questions differ hugely from the guesses that have preceded them.

The Four Papers

1. "Depression Subtyping Based on Evolutionary Psychiatry: Proximate Mechanisms and Ultimate Functions," by Markus Rantala, Severi Luoto, Indrikis Krams, Hasse Karlsson. *Brain, Behavior, and Immunity*, October 16, 2017.[68]
2. "Understanding the genetic contribution of the human leukocyte antigen System to common major psychiatric disorders in a world pandemic context," by Ryad Tamouza, Rajagopal Krishnamoorthy, Marion Leboyer. *Brain, Behavior, and Immunity*, October 5, 2020.[69]
3. "Ketamine blocks bursting in the lateral habenula to rapidly relieve depression," by Yan Yang, Yihui Cui, Kangning Sang, Yiyan Dong, Shuangshuang Ma, Hailan Hu. *Nature*, February 15, 2018.[70]
4. "What Animals Really Think," by Alison Abbott. *Nature*, August 13, 2020.[71]

Evolutionary Psychiatry

Evolutionary psychiatry describes MDD as a "heterogeneous syndrome with patients differing remarkably in symptom profile, pathophysiology and treatment responsiveness."[72] The authors suggest ancient origins of most of the subtypes where each syndrome is born of a given source that produces a syndrome of response composed of ancient "proximate

68 *Markus Rantala, Severi Luoto, Indrikis Krams, and Hasse Karlsson, "De- pression Subtyping Based on Evolutionary Psychiatry: Proximate Mechanisms and Ultimate Functions," Brain, Behavior, and Immunity 69 (March 2018): 603–607.*

69 *Tamouza, "Understanding human leukocyte antigen contribution to psychi- atric disorders," 731–739.*

70 *Yang, "Ketamine blocks bursting in the lateral habenula," 317–322.*

71 *Alison Abbott, "What Animals Really Think," Nature Vol 584 (13 August 2020): 183–185.*

72 *Rantala, "Depression Subtyping Based on Evolutionary Psychiatry," 603–607.*

mechanisms" that evolved long ago to address particular situations with particular needs that the authors define as an "ultimate function." The theory further postulates that often what had evolved originally as an "ultimate function," where it had been a positive adaptation in that hunter–gatherer or early agriculture lifestyle, no longer works owing to the disappearance of those ancient situations in our modern world.

As an example, consider the subtypes of "infection-induced depression" versus "postpartum depression." Chronic infection of many varieties can lead to depression. The cause here is the infection itself. When sick with infection we have devised a variety of adaptations to deal with the illness. One is an incredibly complex immune system to go to war with the pathogens; another is sickness behavior, a system of mood "which includes somatic, cognitive and behavioral changes that help individuals overcome infection by conserving metabolic

resources for the use of the immune system, thus avoiding further infections." Specifically, "sickness behavior includes the symptoms of anorexia, psychomotor retardation, sleep disturbances, anergy, anhedonia, weakness, malaise, listlessness, hyperalgesia and impaired concentration."[73]

Sickness behavior would be termed here a "proximate mechanism" for dealing with the disease. All the changes of the syndrome of sickness behavior are adaptive in that they reduce energy expenditure for use by the immune system as they promote social isolation to reduce new disease exposure. In this subtype, sickness behavior arrives directly by way of the infection, but we see in the other subtypes that the syndrome of depression can itself, without an infectious agent, become the actual agent of stress; all by itself, the depression induces changes in the hypothalamic–pituitary–adrenal (HPA) axis that result in inflammatory dysregulation with increased levels of pro-inflammatory cytokines that, per the theory—all by themselves—induce sickness behavior.

This is in marked contrast to another depression subtype, postpartum depression, where 10–15% of modern mothers suffer a loss of interest in their babies and may try to hurt them. The mothers also typically exhibit symptoms of crying, suicidal ideation, anger and hopelessness, but they do not suffer from an upregulated HPA axis, do not have elevated levels of inflammatory cytokines and have lower salivary stress hormone levels.

---

73 *Rantala, "Depression Subtyping Based on Evolutionary Psychiatry," 603–607.*

Here, the proximate mechanism of the depression is the mother's sense of abandonment by her husband and/ or her local society. The syndrome of postpartum depression does not normally include sickness behavior.[74]

The authors reference the Ayoreo Indians whose lifestyles more closely mirror those of our ancestral conditions and note that infanticide is routinely practiced in their communities on 38% of all babies.[75] Clearly, the modern mother suffering postpartum depression is trying to say something to her allomothers from thousands of years ago, but our modern ears simply cannot hear the message—and if they did hear it—would they address it?

Some could, but the point is the mismatch of ancient Imperatives evolving from ancient times and coming into play during the technology-inspired isolation of our exquisitely lonely modern times. The constant changes always present in modern, dynamic societies often mean that our programmed responses amount to a new language where the words are as inapplicable as they are misunderstood.

The authors define twelve subtypes of depression:

1. Infection-induced depression.
2. Depression induced by long-term stress (previously melancholy).
3. Depression induced by loneliness.
4. Depression induced by traumatic events.
5. Depression induced by hierarchy conflict.
6. Depression induced by grief.
7. Depression induced by romantic rejection.
8. Postpartum depression.
9. Season-related depression.
10. Chemically induced depression.
11. Depression induced by somatic diseases.
12. Starvation-induced depression.

The authors list twelve "proximate mechanisms" for responding to depression.

1. Emotional pain.
2. Proneness for suicide.
3. Rumination.

---

74 *Rantala, "Depression Subtyping Based on Evolutionary Psychiatry," 603–607.*

75 *Rantala, "Depression Subtyping Based on Evolutionary Psychiatry," 603–607.*

4. Change in appetite: significant mass gain or loss.
5. Anhedonia.
6. Sleep disorder.
7. Fatigue.
8. Anxiety.
9. Psychomotor agitation or retardation.
10. Pessimism.
11. Self-accusations.
12. Low self-esteem.

The authors of this evolutionary subtyping approach to depression have certainly expanded our sense of what depression is beyond the concept of a single, uniform entity infesting all brains in the same way. The symptoms are often variable, as are the responses to different modalities of care. Though we are getting more complicated and, therefore, also getting more complete portraits of what is going on—we have not yet addressed anything that might suggest what depression is—beyond something that happens when the pro-inflammatory cytokines increase.

Perusing the list of subtypes, something else jumps out. Hierarchy, romantic, postpartum and grief subtypes are entities whose existences depend upon personal evaluation and assessment of global opportunity before proceeding on to depression, and as such are subject to variable responses from the sufferer. Note that there is an element of choice here, even if that choice is only to decide that the situation is good or bad. This information from the environment processes throughout the brain with special foci in the amygdala, hippocampus and frontal lobes. Somehow, the sufferer contributes to the choice to become depressed; she plays a role in deciding that the world is how she sees it, how she should immediately respond and what brain state is to come next.

In the third paper I investigate depression as a brain state where the LHb at the cellular level is seen to participate in the decision-making that calls upon the programmed brain state of depression as a valid and potentially productive behavior response to environmental stress

The fourth paper goes from intimate—as—intricate laboratory probes and wired voltage meters to a thoroughly modern AI approach where every brain neuron cell—firing is directly monitored and statistically correlated so that the detection of far-flung cells sharing the same networks may be identified and defined.

These last two papers are closely related in that they both try to show us the anatomical neural circuits that are necessary for the induction of brain states, moods and emotions in mice and zebrafish larvae. They both do so utilizing quite different, but equally sophisticated, tools for obtaining their data. But where one seems almost Victorian in its technological rigor and mechanical laboratory skill in dealing with the delicacies of mouse brain, the other manages a nearly magical combination of Xbox, an aquarium and remote sensing to follow and define every individual cell of a zebrafish larva brain as it shifts mental states by changing neural circuits while deciding to snack—or not—on paramecia.

But before we get to that, as well as the answer to that question of "What is, exactly, depression?" more fundamental knowledge about laying the foundations for depression can be found in the second paper, where we witness the profound and very different contribution of the immune system in creating the basis for specific psychiatric illnesses. Though this mechanism undoubtedly dances with the LHb in its more conventional directing of conventional brain states, it is different. Dendritic pruning is not a process of choice; it is as mandatory a process as adolescence itself, though we do not understand its reason for being or its importance. Abnormal dendritic pruning results in a variety of what we might term affliction-type diseases of depression that can range from a light "touch" to full catastrophe.

Neurodevelopmental Psychiatric Disease

Our immune system has been recognized for years as providing fundamental contributions to several organic diseases, thereby defining them as autoimmune. The brief list includes type 1 diabetes, celiac disease, Grave's disease and myasthenia gravis. Technological improvements over the past 20 years have led to such entities as next- generation sequencing (NGS) and genome-wide association studies (GWAS), which have revealed previously unrecognized statistical correlations between causal genes and the diseases created.

The HLA system encodes proteins predominantly responsible for regulating immune and inflammatory processes.

> "Recent data also show that HLAmoleculesmodulate the development and function of the Central Nervous System

> (CNS), including core functions such as neuronal/synaptic plasticity, learning, memory and behaviolr, as well as more direct modulation of neuron–neuron interactions and neuro-signaling ... A deeper exploration of the HLA region further revealed a major contribution to schizophrenia risk mediated by increased complement C4A gene copy number with consequent C4-dependent neuro-synaptic pruning."[76]

This mechanism of disease production, focused as it is on dendritic regulation, applies not only to schizophrenia but, with variations mostly related to the timing of critical viral infections, also to autism spectrum disorder (ASD) and bipolar disorder (BP). The authors also note that MDD and ADHD are underpinned by immuno-inflammatory processes and have therefore been suspected to be products of similar events where dendritic pruning would play a role, but they have found none. Very recent GWAS failed to identify HLA-related signals to either MDD or ADHD. But the authors assert that they remain suspicious and suggest that the so-far negative testing for components of immunity "may reflect the extreme heterogeneity of psychiatric disorders in a highly polygenic context where the MHC/HLA contribution may simply be difficult to unmask."[77]

So, we have the entity of depression described as a product of any of at least twelve evolutionary mechanisms that impose themselves on the organism that is humankind, as well as infectious–immune mechanisms that produce the depression of bipolar disease by way of variable dendritic pruning. And we must accept the possibility that general depression itself might still be in some sense a product of the immune system.

Though we have talked much about the varieties of the soil and the background for producing depression, as well as the fact that choice seems to play a role, we still have not really talked about what it is. We cannot yet "see" depression. But there is visible structure to this variegated thing that is this dark mood, and we are going to see it. By studying the nematode Caenorhabditis elegans, the zebrafish, Danio rerio and the

76 *Tamouza, "Understanding human leukocyte antigen contribution to psychi- atric disorders," 731–739.*

77 *Tamouza, "Understanding human leukocyte antigen contribution to psychi- atric disorders," 731–739.*

"congenitally learned helpless" (CLH) rats of Chinese neuroscience labs, we will finally come to innovative insights on the nature of what we call depression.[78]

The 2018 Nature article, "Ketamine blocks bursting in the lateral habenula to rapidly relieve depression," was a tour de force of then-current technology where mice—genetically altered to be especially susceptible to depression and stress—were fitted with an array of cell-level probes and monitors. The list included—but was not limited to—whole-cell patch clamps for real-time cellular voltage determinations, implanted cannulas capable of administering direct ketamine infusions into either habenula, mass spectroscopy and liquid chromatography to determine dosage at cellular levels, and optogenetic stimulation of habenular signal cells to induce or abate despair.[79]

Through detailed graphs, diagrams and tables and the muted technical descriptions of laboratory rats guided through worlds of scheduled and micro-metered horror, we see many of the biologic components of wide-ranging animal emotionality, and we see how that emotionality is influenced by an induced brain state that originates in the lateral habenula (LHb) as a product of stress. The article suggests a depression paradigm by detailing the neuronal specifics of internal voltage levels and firing rates that determine the nature of the signal—termed the lateral habenular burst mode (LHbM)—sent from the LHb to the rest of the brain, and how that signal then inhibits the brain's reward centers downstream to produce the despair and depression so evident in the mice.[80]

The reward centers observed to respond include the dopaminergic ventral tegmental area (VTA), the serotonergic dorsal raphe nucleus (DRN) and the GABA-ergic rostromedial tegmental nucleus (RMTg). The rats' behavior corresponds dramatically with the LHb signal as despair appears in lockstep with the LHbM, and then abates nearly instantly with infusions of ketamine. This article, through complicated tables and graphs, demonstrates the induction of despair through signaling initiated in the LHb, and then we see reversal of the rats' despair with the

---

78 *Joao C. Marques, Meng Li, Diane Schaak, Drew N. Robson, and Jennifer M. Li, "Internal State Dynamics Shape Brain-Wide Activity and Foraging Behavior," Nature (December 18, 2019).*

79 *Yang, "Ketamine blocks bursting in the lateral habenula," 317–322.*

80 *Yang, "Ketamine blocks bursting in the lateral habenula," 317–322.*

administration of ketamine and subsequent abatement of the LHbM. The paper is foundational and key to understanding the induction of at least some varieties of depression.[81]

But we are not yet able to visualize this disease. Technology, however, will again lift us to another level in getting to a more complete view of depression in particular and of brain states in general. It is the structure of the brain state that we are looking for in our quest to understand depression.

In another Nature magazine article by Alison Abbott—appearing two years after Yang's paper of high-tech cellular-level patch-clamps that defined the LHbM and ketamine's role in abating it—other researchers enjoyed an entirely different project. Their description and participation in the experiment, compared to the previous study with all its researcher-placed clamps and probes, sounds more like a spectator sport.

"Using tracking microscopy to monitor whole-brain neuronal activity at cellular resolution in freely moving zebrafish larvae, we show the zebrafish spontaneously alternate between two persistent internal states during foraging for live prey (Paramecia). We image whole-brain calcium activity at cellular resolution in freely swimming zebrafish larvae expressing pan-neuronal H2B-GCaMP6s during foraging and extracted the florescence across time F(t) for each neuronal centroid in the brain using non-negative matrix factorization (NMF)."[82]

The platform allowed them to view every cell in the larvae's brains while the creatures—barely the size of an eyelash—swim freely in a 35-millimeter-diameter dish of water, snacking on their microscopic prey.[83]

Being able to track every cell in the brain changes things. In the article by Yang and colleagues, the study was based on numerical measures of cellular voltages, patterns of electrical firing, and comparison to coincident events in structures downstream from the LHb. The figures were then correlated to both measured ketamine concentrations and despair-associated behavior. The study was detailed, extremely technical and difficult. It was also groundbreaking.

Equally ground-breaking but sleek and slick in its modernity, in the

---

81 *Yang, "Ketamine blocks bursting in the lateral habenula," 317–322.*

82 *Abbott, "What Animals Really Think," 183–185.*

83 *Abbott, "What Animals Really Think," 183–185.*

aquarium study we watch and record the firings of every brain neuron from a distance on millisecond timescales as the free-swimming zebrafish larvae go about a relatively normal existence feeding on Paramecia. Everything that follows, then, is statistical as mountains of data are analyzed to define the relationships between cells—all of them—such that networks that reach to many and distant parts of the brain can be identified in their entirety and their components analyzed to understand their complicated interrelationships.[84]

Neural networks are constructed of interacting, task-oriented components. Brain states are products of neural networks. In the LHbM article, a network was implied but, beyond a few named components, it remained hidden.[85] But, after exhaustive statistical analysis involving artificial intelligence, machine learning and new mathematical tools, these become the first photographs of an entire neural network visible as we have never seen them before. Neurons that fire together—or in a particular sequence that defines them as related—are recognized as wiring together by way of the statistics whose algorithms reveal the networks in dramatic detail and activity. During different brain states, we see that every component on the network is micro-optimized to respond in a unique way, assumedly defined by the network's manipulations over the course of the organism's evolution.

In this article studying zebrafish larvae, the authors study the distribution of network neurons that determine the transitions from the mental states of "exploration"—where the larva are swimming freely and covering larger distances—and "exploitation," where the animal inhibits locomotion and pursues the prey using specific techniques not used in the other mental state, such as eye convergence, high-precision turns, capture swims and ingestion maneuvers.[86]

Utilizing the tool of linear regression, the authors identify a distributed network of neurons triggered at the moment of transition from exploration to exploitation. The neural clusters are focused in the ventrolateral habenula, the dorsal raphe and two other clusters. Note that the zebrafish are utilizing the same brain modules as the mice utilized in the preceding article in producing their despair responses.[87]

---

84 *Abbott, "What Animals Really Think," 183–185.*

85 *Yang, "Ketamine blocks bursting in the lateral habenula," 317–322.*

86 *Abbott, "What Animals Really Think," 183–185.*

87 *Abbott, "What Animals Really Think," 183–185.*

From fish to mice —a fair stretch on the evolutionary timeline— the LHb continues to be an organ concerned with the changing of significant brain states. Is the LHb then likely to execute the same function in humans? In a review article of the habenular nuclei in the *Philosophical Transactions of the Royal Society*, the authors noted that the medial habenula (MHb) "appears to be conserved in all vertebrate species that have been examined," but that in comparison, "the LHb shows broader and less evolutionarily conserved conductivity."[88]

Overall, then, we have in this zebrafish article a dramatic revealing of mental processes—namely, brain networks defining brain states— that in turn reprogram the individual neurons on the network to perform in a team fashion. These networks and brain states work on many different levels and over many different time spans. In zebrafish the mental states are few but well defined. Moving up the evolutionary ladder to bigger and badder brains means far more complexity and variety, but also far more function and applicability to a changing world.

We watched zebrafish utilize the LHb to send a periodic signal out to the dorsal raphe, where neurons defining "exploitation behavior" took over to initiate hunting maneuvers. Then, much higher on the evolutionary ladder, the "congenitally learned helpless" rats put their lateral habenulae to work sending out LHbMs to their dorsal raphes, but now the message sent by the new brain state is not to eat Paramecia, but rather to contain all reward centers and go into a mode of depression.

So, what is depression, exactly? Depression is a fashioned mental state that is a collection of behaviors that have evolved over many generations in repeated response to perceived varieties of thwarted ambition. Depression, and brain states in general, are based on semi-malleable templates that stand ready to be called upon. Anatomically, it is a collection of distributed brain modules that together produce a programmed system of emotional responses that originally evolved to deal with a particular state of thwarted ambition but—with subsequent environmental and societal changes—may no longer effectively deal with the situation in a positive way and, in fact, may contribute to situations of pathology.

But depression can also be a product of dendritic pruning in the entirely different syndrome of bipolar disease. In bipolar disease—a

---

88 Bianco, "Habenular Nuclei," 106.

disease of primary affliction—does choice play a role at all similar to the mechanisms involving choice as defined in evolutionary psychiatry? We do not know yet.

What are the characteristics of a brain state? For that answer, Allison Abbot interviewed Cal Tech's David Anderson and Ralph Adolphs for ideas on what the necessary characteristics of a neural circuit producing a brain state would be. From an article not mentioned, they listed the following:

1. **Persistence**. A mental state must outlast the stimulus that was its trigger. This component is key, highly variable and defines the difference between many brain states.
2. **Generalizability**, meaning that different triggers can initiate the same or similar states.
3. **Scalability**, meaning that different triggers bring various levels of response.[89]

This could certainly apply to depression, just as it could to anxiety, love, fear, thirst or the love songs of male fruit flies. Does this mean that the brain state of depression has the same general type of anatomic structure—though with different distributions and connections—as the state of thirst, or possibly the emotions associated with identity theft? It probably does, but they will have vastly different histories, time constraints, stimuli and anatomic neuronal tracts as revealed in the following scenarios.

Thirst is, of course, among the very oldest of those emotions for land-dwellers, related as it is to the regulation of the fluids our body needs to stay alive. This mechanism has been evolving for hundreds of millions of years and has been fine-tuned in every organism our DNA has evolutionarily passed through to warn us when in need of fluids or salts. We have evolved multiple sensors to inform us of those needs and have an organ, the lamina terminalis, where most of the information from those sensors is collated before fine-tuning the individual modules of the thirst network from which will emanate one possibility from a measured variety of "thirst mental states." Depending upon our level of thirst, the organism will direct itself to available modes of refreshment. This implies that every neurologic module of the thirst network will be

---

89 *Abbott, "What Animals Really Think," 183–185.*

optimized to reflect the appropriate differences between a teen sipping soda at the beach and Fred C. Dobbs dying of thirst in the Sierra Madre.

At close to the opposite end of the persistence measure of brain states would be suites of emotions related to transient events of everyday life—such as identity theft—which are unlikely to make permanent inroads to our brain circuitry as they would with more necessary concerns. Unlike the incessant thirst problem, hunter-gatherers knew little of identity theft.

Though there are certainly foundational emotions that we are born with, most of the learned library of emotions that accompany us through life are created by us in a fashion similar to that of identity theft. Some level of actual firsthand experience of the emotion creates it, such as having a credit card misused by mysterious entities. The emotions experienced at the time will be remembered: the lost money will be suffered, efforts to understand and avoid the nature of the fraud will be pursued, the mistakes made will be reviewed and behavior will be altered. That suite of memories and associated emotions will be stored as a neural network that will be stimulated to various degrees in the future as situations arise that recall the event.

But this variety of mental state barely compares to the portrait of thirst, either in its level of presence or its importance to the organism. Our brains deal with "little" problems like theft constantly and do not need to biologically alter the organism to ensure survival for it—at least not yet. But water has shaped every piece of our existence since the dawn of our time on the planet, and our bodies and minds have shaped themselves to answer those constant and consequential needs.

Between these two mental states defined as polar extremes by their complexity and biologic importance, would fall depression. It certainly satisfies Anderson's qualifying list of persistence, generalizability and scalability. Though no specific organ that we yet recognize is devoted to depression in the same way that the lamina terminalis and its associated sensors are hardwired to thirst, the LHb or some other complex of neurons will probably turn out to be defined in a manner that suggests an evolved specificity.

But the timing of these two networks is, as we would expect, quite different. The brain state of thirst is a constant and necessary measuring with huge differences in behavior possible for the many different scenarios. But depression is much less needy; it sits waiting like a snake that may need to feed only a few times in a lifetime, or it may come out only once to stay as it engulfs itself in a brain state that is forever.

We create many of our emotions, but the most critical we are born with. Dealing with identity theft is important to a modern citizen, but it is not usually critical to existence. Depressions come programmed through the genetics of the organism, but every variety requires a specific type of introduction, after which the particular variety of depression may stay or go. But thirst is as constantly necessary as the rising sun and will always be present in any of a variety of wardrobes, ranging from a late afternoon sipping of tea to a desperate gulping by the previously mentioned Mr. Dobbs.

All three—thirst, identity theft and depression—utilize monitored brain states dependent upon neural networks constructed of optimizable components that in turn produce responses whose designs were originally meant to enhance survival and adaptation. Thirst still does. Identity theft creates emotions and moods in a game played on the fly where some do better than others; it provides a model of mood that arguably applies to all of our emotions.

But depression is a little different. The negative mood might be something selected for in some of the evolutionary scenarios—if postpartum depression elicits help, it may be defined as a benefit in that the baby's chance of survival might be increased. Applying the same evolutionary logic to any psychological stressor—from lack of rock star status to severe political repression—may define an instance of thwarted ambition where depression becomes a preferred option to be selected for in preference to a world that has denied an individual the lifestyle that her brain believes itself destined to lead.

As discussed, this decision may not have been a conscious choice, but know that that individual's frontal lobes were unquestionably talking to her amygdala and hippocampus about every one of her perceived-as-possible futures.

CHAPTER 5

The Neolithic Y-Chromosome Bottleneck and the Origins of Depression

At a recent national conference for ketamine physicians one of the presenters spent two hours giving a list of proposed contributors to depression. The lengthy list was composed mostly of psychologic, physiologic and physical assaults to the person or her neurology that could result in depression. Depression, then, was being presented as "damage" to the organism, something untoward that, if avoided, would not lead to the undesirable state.

In Andrew Solomon's brilliant work on depression, *"The Noonday Demon,"* he asks, "Is depression a derangement, like cancer, or can it be defensive, like nausea?" Could it be more than just an unfortunate consequence of random events? He then notes that depression involves mechanisms that may have reproductive advantage even though those advantages are not obvious.

After all, if a guy is depressed and that depression inflicts upon him a brain that simply does not think as well in its depressed state as it does when it's free of depression, and his memory is likewise compromised, and he is antisocial, his blood pressure is high and his diabetes is out of control, why would the cheerleader want that guy?

Well, she doesn't. So, how can we explain that depression seems to be selected for in a situation where every one of its components would seem to predict powerfully undesirable influences on reproduction?

Mr. Solomon proposes four possibilities that would allow for depression to be naturally selected for.

1. "Depression served a purpose in evolution's pre-human times that it no longer serves."
2. "The stresses of modern life are incompatible with the brains we have evolved, and depression is a consequence of our doing what we did not evolve to do"

3. "Depression serves a useful function in human society, and it is sometimes a good thing for people to be depressed."
4. "The genes and consequent biological structures that are implicated in depression are also implicated in other, more useful behaviors or feelings. Depression is a secondary result of a useful variant in brain physiology."

The big question here, I think, asks whether depression is simply a product of misfortune, of damage to what should be a more normal personality, or is it some kind of potentially desirable partner of behavior that, if understood, might be dealt with in a more productive way than we are currently managing? If it is selected for, might that not have implications in the focus of our efforts for both treatment and our general attitude toward the disease?

What is the evidence that might suggest that depression is, in fact, an evolutionarily selected-for entity?

1. Depression travels among many families in a manner that suggests a genetic component.
2. Depression shows a 3 to 1 female preponderance, suggesting a possible genetic role, though it is quite clear that at least some of the proclivity for females can be explained through the mechanisms of estrogen.
3. The lateral habenula's role in depression and despair, as described in the February 15, 2018 issue of *Nature* magazine, makes absolutely clear that depression is a state selected for by evolution. After all, the lateral habenula is an actual, genetically defined brain organ that induces a state of despair or depression when behaviorally stimulated with stress. Though there are undoubtedly many factors both psychological and physiological that can influence depression, the lateral habenula and its signal, the lateral habenular burst mode, are creatures produced by evolution; this has many practical and philosophic consequences far beyond this paper.

So, back to the cheerleader and why she might select that depressed guy for a mate? For that answer we must ask a big question: where in all of history can we find a situation where depression makes reproduction more likely? What situation could possibly convert the monumental passivity and helplessness that is depression into something that might qualify for the happy reproductive success of a Mr. Saturday Night?

One possibility stands out above all others and, in fact, reduces the "all others" to lesser versions of itself. This entity not only explains depression but also explains most of the basic social structures that are important for society to exist, such as our sense of hierarchy and our allegiance to national entities as opposed to familial ones. It also explains the development of the concept of money, of war and of Donald Trump.

The entity of which I speak is the Neolithic Y-Chromosome Bottleneck, a current internet meme much discussed in the past couple of years. The graph accompanying this meme reveals that every society that has experienced the development of agriculture went through a 2000 to 3000-year period of time *where all of our grandfathers consistently and thoroughly raped all of our grandmothers.*

Now, the word "rape" might not be exactly appropriate, but there was a man of kingly stature in all of our pasts from whom we are all descended that demanded exclusive insemination rights for himself; all wombs were to be opened and filled exclusively by appendages of the king. During this time, only one in 17 men got to father a child; all of the other men were non-reproductive, either enslaved or killed.

Every agricultural society went through this sexual enslavement.

How could this Neolithic Y-Chromosome Bottleneck, as depressing as it is, lead to the evolution of depression as a recurrent and extremely common disease?

At the beginnings of agriculture, 10 to 12,000 years ago, there was no history because there was no writing, so we have few details of those times. But what we do know of that period would allow us to point to the story of Moses and the Medianites as an illustrative example.

Moses went to war with the Medianites over the worship of Baal, a fertility God. His generals returned to announce to Moses that they had won, that they had already killed all the men, and that the women had all been brought back for distribution among his followers. Moses famously announced that a Medianite woman who had been with a Medianite man would be as a mote in the eye or a thorn in the side, such that all non-virgins must be killed. This was done.

But those Copper Age Neolithic kings would not likely have been concerned about any captured women and their virgin status, at least not in the same sense that Moses did. What these early kings needed were soldiers, soldiers preferably in the physical image and with the aggressive mind set of the warrior king himself.

These early human societies that were for the first time exceeding the Hunter-Gatherer maximum of 300 humans per functional unit, knew life and death imperatives that directed their concerns. Those early kings knew with rapt focus that they had to grow enough food to grow enough people to make enough in the way of farming tools and living structures to allow for the production of military equipment and the training of soldiers such that, if a Moses and his army showed up on the neighboring mesa, they would not be immediately extinguished. This was the way of society and status in the Neolithic.

In this situation of a dire need for arm-strong soldiers, perhaps it was an effective strategy for that undoubtedly arm-strong warrior king to do all of the inseminating. If so, what was in the mind of that warrior king who was great, great, great grandfather to us all as he came to visit the great, great, great grandmothers that gave birth to us all? Did he bring Great Great Great Grandmother a rose because she was about to make him a soldier? Or did he have hope for some sport through her resistance?

The answer is, yes.

And Grandmother? What was in Grandmother's mind here? This is important because this is the moment where depression evolved. The key concept here is thwarted ambition. We mentioned above that depression must have a function; after all, the lateral habenula is an evolutionarily evolved, naturally selected for organ. There are reasons for its appearance as certain as opposable thumbs and happy, nutrition- oriented breasts.

As a concubine of the king or one of his high lords, Grandma's job was to make twenty soldiers. No options. But Grandma would not have been into this. Women had very effectively ruled most of human evolution for the previous 6 million years. If we look at diversity in the human male chromosome for those 6 million years, we see not the 1:17 ratio of the copper age kings, but rather a 1:2 ratio. Here, as Hunter-Gatherers on the Serengeti, only 50% of men got to father children. This constraint on male sexuality was directed by the female; if you as a guy were too short, hairy or stupid you weren't allowed into the intimate folds of femalia that led to children.

So, when Grandma is taken from her home on the Serengeti and placed in that Neolithic king's harem, is she going to make that king 20 soldiers just because he asks or tells her to? I would think not. In fact, she's likely to be furious with it. After all, we all know from our own Mason-Dixon Line experiences just what happens to an uppity slave; they are killed, or at least brutalized.

Making those 20 soldiers instead of wandering the Serengeti in her most favored Hunter-Gatherer existence might very well be one of the ultimate examples of thwarted ambition. As such, it is also very high on the list of opportunities for depression to be naturally selected for.

Consider:

Grandma who won't make soldiers = DEAD
Grandma who will make soldiers = DEPRESSED + 20 children
who carry the willing-to-be-depressed gene.

If we assume, then, that Grandma's choice to have those 20 soldiers and to accept her depression led to the modification of her lateral habenula that produced the proclivity for depression in her offspring, are there similar, identifiable instances of thwarted ambition leading to depression and anxiety in our world?

A quote I once heard might contribute insight into this question. The quote asserted that there are only four jobs worth having: president, movie star, sports star, rock star. Though an obviously elitist comment, I would assert that the quote doesn't need to come from any particular person to reveal validity. Consider that any teen with a smart phone watching the lives of the rich and famous while swaying to his favorite hip-hop dude, knows painfully that he himself is not only not president, a movie star, a sports star or a rock star, but that he will NEVER be president, a movie star, a sports star or a rock star.

I would assert that that teen is right in there with Grandma in her Neolithic harem suffering a very well-defined sense of thwarted ambition. This world of growing wealth disparity, population growth, global warming and cold Civil War is anything but a welcoming one. *Anxiety, depression and PTSD as disease statistics are growing in every demographic group in our society, but they are far and away the most extreme with our teens* where the smart phone has conspired with the shifting instability of adolescence to create the constraints of depression that emanate directly from all of our lateral habenulae.

We are only beginning to define this problem and are finding as we do get a peek at it that the medical world is functionally looking the other way for reasons that are more financial than medical. Dealing with this problem will require major changes in the economics of psychiatry as we continue to gather information to define this as yet very undefined entity.

PART II

KETAMINE CONFIDENTIAL: PROFESSIONAL MURDER AND FRAUD AND SNAKES, OH MY!

CHAPTER 6

A Scale of Human Happiness Opening: Why This Matters

Within a single week, several stories landed differently for me than they ever had before. Watching a Rolling Stones documentary—again—I found myself thinking about Brian Jones and realizing, with a kind of stunned clarity, *I might* have been able to save him. Then Anderson Cooper spoke publicly about his mother's lifelong trauma, and the same thought returned. Even an old friend who took his own life years ago drifted back into my mind, not as an abstract tragedy but as a clinical possibility.

"If only I had known then what I know today about ketamine, I could have saved them."

That sentence, repeated and unpolished, reflects not narcissism but shock—the shock of discovering that a disease long treated as intractable may, in fact, be rapidly and reliably reversible.

The Barbarism of PreKetamine Depression Care

Before ketamine, treatment for severe, ongoing depression was both crude and remarkably ineffective. Antidepressants were—and remain—only marginally better than placebo for most patients. Worse, they often increase suicidality early in treatment. These concerns were not theoretical. In the case of Prozac, Eli Lilly selectively published favorable trials while discarding nearly half the data, without denting the drug's $10billion annual revenues.

Over four decades in emergency medicine, I have seen thousands of profoundly depressed patients enter the emergency department and leave unchanged—still flattened, still suffering, still dangerous to themselves. Depression is psychiatry's primary mandate: cure it and you restore a fully functioning citizen. Fail, and you leave behind a person trapped in relentless psychic pain, often contemplating selfdestruction as the only imaginable exit.

Many psychiatric illnesses can be managed but not cured. Schizophrenia and autism may improve, but normalcy remains out of reach. Depression, however, is different. Ketamine has revealed that this particular disease—affecting otherwise intact, often brilliant minds—is not only treatable but rapidly reversible.

Ketamine: A Standard Candle for the Mind

Ketamine is as close to a miracle drug as psychiatry has ever encountered. Unlike SSRIs, it does not merely dull symptoms or shift perception. It restores normalcy—sometimes within hours. Patients do not merely report feeling "a bit better"; they return to joy, clarity, and cognitive flexibility so unmistakable that no clinician or patient could miss the transformation.

In astronomy, distant objects are measured using "standard candles"—objects of known brightness that allow us to estimate vast distances. Ketamine functions similarly for depression. By abruptly lifting the illness, it reveals the true depth of suffering that preceded it. Only when depression vanishes can its magnitude be appreciated.

A physician who has not witnessed ketamine's effects has not seen the defining clinical event of modern psychiatry.

Depression Is Not Sadness

Depression is not simply extreme unhappiness. It is not situational despair, nor a moral failing, nor a weakness of will. It is a disease that hijacks the very machinery of motivation, meaning, and hope. The same brain capable of genius becomes inert, joyless, and exquisitely painful.

Most people will never experience this disease. But 5–12% of Americans will—roughly 30–40 million individuals at any given time, with women disproportionately affected. Add PTSD, and nearly 50 million Americans suffer from mental illnesses that are directly responsive to ketamine.

Despite this, the vast majority are treated with medications shown to be ineffective for mild and moderate depression. Until recently, that failure was tolerated because there was nothing better. Ketamine changed that—and in doing so, exposed the inadequacy of the status quo.

Constructing a Scale of Happiness

Happiness is subjective, but that does not make it meaningless. Human beings constantly assess their own wellbeing, and those assessments drive every major decision we make. While no machine can measure happiness, we can still conceptualize it.

Let us imagine a scale:

0: Average mental state (Freud's "normal misery").
+100: Sustained joy—life working as intended.
–200: A bitter divorce.
–400: The death of a child.

Major depression does not sit neatly on this scale. It exceeds it. By definition, it introduces thoughts of selfharm, existential collapse, and cognitive paralysis. Its suffering rivals—and often exceeds—historical atrocities, not in circumstance but in *experienced pain.*

The Moral Math

There are currently tens of millions of Americans living with untreated or inadequately treated major depression. Ketamine has been known for years to relieve this suffering in a large majority of patients, yet access remains limited—often cashonly, often prohibitively expensive, and frequently discouraged by academic psychiatry.

Why?

Because ketamine is inexpensive, offpatent, difficult to monetize, and disruptive to a pharmaceutical model built on daily pills with marginal efficacy. SSRIs remain enormously profitable. Ketamine threatens that revenue.

This is not negligence. It is structural indifference.

Psychiatry's Crisis of Courage

Psychiatry has been slow to adopt ketamine for practical reasons—it is injectable, requires monitoring, and falls outside the specialty's pillbased comfort zone. But those challenges are solvable. What is harder to justify is the continued allegiance to pharmaceutical narratives that downplay ketamine's value while exaggerating its risks.

The result is patient abandonment: millions left to suffer when a powerful treatment exists.

Emerging Science, Present Reality

Recent research has clarified ketamine's mechanism of action. Its antidepressant effects arise not from anesthesia but from rapid synaptogenesis and enhanced neuroplasticity mediated by AMPA receptors and downstream pathways such as mTOR and BDNF. This "braingrowing" effect explains both its speed and its potency.

Future drugs may replicate these effects orally and without side effects—but they are years away. Ketamine exists now. It is inexpensive, effective, and deployable with modern technology.

A Call to Ethical Medicine

If ketamine were widely available:

Patients would recover.

Productivity would increase.

Suffering would plummet.

The only barrier is institutional inertia reinforced by profit.

Health care cannot be governed solely by market logic. When financial incentives perpetuate suffering rather than relieve it, medicine loses its moral compass.

Ketamine forces a reckoning. It reveals both the true depth of depression—and the cost of ignoring it.

References (Chicago Manual of Style)

Turner, Eric H., et al. "Selective Publication of Antidepressant Trials and Its Influence on Apparent Efficacy." *New England Journal of Medicine* 358, no. 3 (2008): 252–260.

Shafer, Arthur. "Biomedical Conflicts of Interest: A Defence of the Sequestration Thesis." *Journal of Medical Ethics* 30, no. 1 (2004): 8–24.

Fournier, Jay C., et al. "Antidepressant Drug Effects and Depression Severity." *JAMA* 303, no. 1 (2010): 47–53.

Ramo, Joshua Cooper. *The Age of the Unthinkable.* New York: Little, Brown and Company, 2009.

Castrén, Eero. "How Do Antidepressants Work?" Lecture, University of Helsinki, 2015.

Pittenger, Christopher, and Ronald S. Duman. "Stress, Depression, and Neuroplasticity." *Neuropsychopharmacology* 32 (2007): 88–109.

CHAPTER 7

Depression's Greatest Lie

In that ketamine suppression has been a nation-wide theme for the past 20 years, I would assert that major value can be gained by heeding the cautionary component of this tale; though this is a mental health story, it is mental health caught in the gears of capitalism to distort and bleed as certainly as any young hand devoured by the butcher's meat grinder. There are billions of dollars that stand to be "lost" in the next few years if ketamine should replace SSRIs and SNRIs. As has been the case in the past, significant effort will be expended to protect those billions.

This means that Big Pharma has great direct monetary incentive to suppress ketamine in a variety of a sad-as-desperate "hide the horse, sell them the donkey" scenario. But in this darker-than-just-embarrassing situation, cold-as-crisp money determines that both Big Pharma and psychiatry would prefer that the horse be killed – much more on this to come.

Immediately below Big Pharma on the great pharmaceutical economic ladder, is academic medicine where we do not see the same lusty concern with the direct sales of pharmaceuticals that so excites and makes hungry the cavernous big bellies of Big Pharma, but there is still enormous money extending boney fingers toward academic medicine and corrupting the process in the form of the donation of new chemistry buildings, new hospital wings, academic travel adventures and the like.

There is nothing intrinsically wrong with wealthy industrial donors giving things to centers of academia; in a general sense, I encourage it strongly. But farther down the line where we see the actual practice of medicine, the practitioners, therapists, and psychiatrists are aware that this cash flow becomes problematic. These are the very people who are supposed to be the ones making decisions that are in the interests of their patients' mental health, but if we compare SSRIs or SNRI's to ketamine, we see a multiplied antidepressant effect of 25-30 times with ketamine, meaning that ketamine is at least 25-30 times as effective as Prozac in relieving depression.

Additionally, ketamine is far safer than other available antidepressants.

If ketamine is truly 25-30 times as effective as SSRIs and SNRIs, why aren't those advocates advocating for the product that works? The reason is actually quite simple: it's not made available to them in their local Mental Health Industrial Complex because it's off-label.

An off-label status can be corrected for a product that is as safe and uniquely effective as ketamine, but it's an expensive and bulky process that focuses the pain on the psychiatrist and the pharmaceutical company – only the patient and society immediately gain from ketamine's being set free. There will be mouthing in the psychiatric bureaucracy about ketamine's being off-label, but the diabetes, hypertension, dry mouth, and diminished sexuality of SSRIs reduce those complaints from psychiatry to a grossly self-serving whining that in turn earns for itself the contempt in Upton Sinclair's observation that: "It is difficult to get a man to understand something when his salary depends on his not understanding it."

If academic medicine genuinely wishes to see normal ketamine made on-label for depression, it will happen in an instant.

This is a major assertion that I'm making on a critically important and sophisticated topic. The subtleties of the antidepressant assertions by Big Pharma and academic medicine have been as misleading as they have been incomplete since Prozac first forced its way onto the scene in 1989.

You pretty much must be a mental health professional to understand the subtleties, which means that often *only the physicians know enough to actually know that they are guilty of not adequately treating their patients* when they have the opportunity.

Even from the inside, though, Big Pharma has been extremely devious. Anne Harrington revealed in her book, "*Mind Fixers,*" both that psychiatry's current medicines do not work, and that their means of studying and defining psychiatric disease is fatally flawed. After all, the source of all psychiatric truth, the DSM-5, relies on simple lists of symptoms whose confirmed attachment to any disease in question has never been defined, proven or validated.

Until Anne Harrington revealed Big Pharma's moneyed, on-going, anti-depressant deceptions, even mental health professionals had limited abilities to recognize the ineffectiveness of the meds.

So, if mental health professionals can't be expected to understand the subtleties of their product, legal officials certainly can't be expected to understand much of the sophisticated arguments relating to SSRIs versus ketamine, or the arguments surrounding the questions of "anesthesia" at low-dose ketamine administration levels. Members of the legal community are guardians of their own profession, but it is generally understood and accepted that they depend upon guidance from medical practitioners when navigating sophisticated medical shores.

For the past four years, DOPL - Utah's Department Of Professional Licensing - has allowed itself to be misdirected across an entire continent of ketamine for depression and ketamine for anesthesia misinformation. Tim Hibler, the DOPL investigator, spent much time conferring with physicians at the University Ketamine Clinic, getting questions and criticisms from them, and then returning to me and trying to decide whether or not "anesthesia was being committed." But the subject has been effectively dropped. One of the stipulations does mention ketamine anesthesia, but the subject has taken a backseat.

In fact, *there is simply no valid accusation even present.* No specific laws are ever mentioned: in our situation here, to break a law requires that an initial written statute be broken. None of the initial stipulations can satisfy this requirement.

I had planned to show this lack of substance – this lack of any essence of illegality - at trial, but the proceeding came to a rather ghastly end when the judge demanded that *my trial* - alone in all of Utah, including murder trials - *should go forward at the height of the pandemic.*

The *judge* even announced at the time that, because his desk was more than 6 feet away from the counselors, *that he would not be wearing a mask.*

I considered this offering of Judge Dibb to be a death threat then, and I continue to consider it a death threat at this moment. I, of course, refused to go to trial in that environment, not least because many other citizens would also have been uniquely exposed if my trial were to have gone forward.

I signed the stipulations and am now setting up the awkward DOPL probation mechanism in which my medical activities will be restructured over the next 1.5-3 years as they will be overseen by another physician, a "supervisor."

> But that has taken a dark turn also, where I now find myself on newly unstable legal ground defined by the

following two notes. The first is a simple memorialization of a meeting that I had with DOPL where, for whatever intention, the meeting was obviously meant to be an attack ambush.

A Memorialization of the Events of the DOPL Probation Meeting of 1-21-2021 for Robert C. Hiemstra, M.D.

On the morning of January 21, 2021, I was looking for my email notification of the scheduled DOPL meeting. I did not find it, but the phone rang and it was from someone at the meeting. We could not get a normal Zoom connection going and so I took the meeting on my cellphone.

I was bright and cheery because, after five months, I had finally obtained a doctor that would satisfy the supervisor requirements of my probation. I had expected the same from the DOPL members.

I was asked generally how things were going, and I responded that not much was going on because of the combination of Covid which kept me at home, and the agreements which kept me from working at medicine. I related that the only thing that I had done was to inform the staff through my office manager that the nurse practitioners now had access to the latest DSM 5 app which, I added, made conventional diagnostics more accessible.

"What?" said a voice, accusatory and with anger in it, "You were practicing medicine despite the stipulations that you signed last September?

Please note that I was on my cellphone where the other end of the line had more than a dozen people who could cut in with comments. I do not know their names and did not record the event, so the quotations are not exact, and the names are all confused. But the statements – and certainly the angry tone – are as accurate as my memory will allow.

The theme of the moment in that meeting was that the members were asserting that my behavior was leading to a situation which might end my medical license and my medical clinic. Now, my presence at this meeting came very specifically as the result of an agreement between DOPL and I that constituted a legal contract. The agreement was that maintenance of my license – and by extension, my clinic – depended upon my completing the terms of a period of probation. As such, fulfilling the terms of the stipulations precluded arbitrarily confiscating my license which, if it then occurred, would constitute a fundamental violation of a sacred contract.

"No, not at all. I don't leave the house and haven't been to the clinic in months," I answered.

"But you were talking with your nurse practitioners, giving them advice," asserted a stern voice.

"The totality of my conversation was with my office manager. I told him to inform the staff that they had access to the latest DSM-5 app. I never spoke to any of the staff."

"Speaking with your staff is practicing medicine," said a female voice sternly.

"But I didn't really speak with them," I said, "just the office manager, and… "

"That is practicing medicine," said another voice.

"Come on," I pleaded, "no one would say that a phone call to the office manager about an app's availability…"

"That's practicing medicine, Doctor."

"Well, I would certainly disagree with you on that, the definition of practicing medicine, but *if you did want to define it that way, I would be happy to conform*. But I would need to know…"

"I'm worried about the safety of the public here," intruded a new voice. "I'm not sure this license should be continued. This clinic is dangerous."

Generally flabbergasted, and quieted by assertive anger, I tried to assert the total compliance that I had thought my presentation of a psychiatric supervisor would produce.

I tried to begin a sentence, "I came here this morning totally willing to comply with the program…" but I was cut off.

"A $500 fine is in order."

"Well, you can certainly do anything you want, but I must say that I simply don't agree."

"All those in favor."

They all apparently agreed.

This second note is a response letter that I had considered distributing to important personnel in, and outside, the DOPL legal structure. Conversation with my attorneys directed me to contain the letter out of concern that it would anger personnel and simply continue the escalation of hostility that is so evident in the note's cataloging of events.

The list of involved personalities is as follows:

Dan Lau	DOPL prosecuting attorney.
Tim Hibler	DOPL inspector.
Larry Gooch	DOPL administrator above Tim Hibler.
Judge Bruce Dibb	DOPL judge overseeing trial of Robert C. Hiemstra.
Greg Soderberg	UMIA attorney assigned to case of Robert C. Hiemstra.

Unsent letter to DOPL Regarding Probation Meeting for Robert C. Hiemstra on 1-21-2021.

Dan Lau was right. This case has insufficient merit and ought to be dropped.

I believe that a reading of my "Memorialization of the Events of the 1-21-21 DOPL Probation Meeting" makes abundantly clear that the board members intended to make cancellation of my medical license, and therefore my clinic, a distinct and likely possibility. This very obvious intention constitutes a violation of the substance of the implied contract that came from the earlier signing of the body of stipulations. As such, the goals of this meeting must be defined as violations of the contract that I signed.

But before this DOPL board is allowed to unilaterally relitigate this sacred contract, let us review the series of past DOPL disgraces that have brought me here.

Firstly, one of my attorneys, Greg Soderberg, communicated to me that at a recent decision-making point in the complexities that related to Covid and whether or not to prosecute, Dan Lau – the chief prosecutor of my case - approached Larry Gooch, a man of the DOPL hierarchy, with the possibility of dropping the case for general lack of merit. He did not see much substance in the remaining complaint.

Mr. Gooch allegedly responded with the comment, "We need to make sure he keeps using those Caretaker Monitors. Leave him on probation."

This is a response that simply makes no medical sense. Patients love the Caretaker Monitor's lack of intrusion, which is an unavoidable annoyance in most other monitors, and it *should be noted that this intrusion is especially obnoxious during the peak moment of dissociation during the ketamine experience.* The staff loves them for providing real-time vital signs for every patient at every nursing station computer, along with real-time video of every patient. All data is stored in the cloud.

And, of primary significance, *they are already paid for; I couldn't return them if I wanted to.*

This statement of Mr. Gooch's is one more in a long list of DOPL musings that demonstrate no knowledge of the medicine involved, and begs the question of what, exactly, is their motivation.

Dan Lau was absolutely right; there is little merit in the issues of this case.

Secondly, the stipulations that I signed have never been discussed or agreed to. There has never been a back-and-forth conversation where we agreed on a single infraction or error in care. It simply never happened.

No tort. No medical errors.

The primary reason that I signed those stipulations came from my personal vulnerability to the functional death threat presented by Judge Bruce Dibb.

The original trial date was March 21, 2021, but was postponed for the pandemic. As communicated to me by my attorney Greg Soderberg, the rescheduled trial date of mid-September 2021, was to be maintained; *the trial would be held.*

Judge Dibb allegedly asked about why my trial should be postponed, despite the fact that *all other trials in the state of Utah – including murder trials – were being delayed for Covid concerns.*

The judge also announced that, because he was going to be more than 6 feet from other people in the courtroom, *he was not going to wear a mask.* Aerosol studies and common sense would now recognize that situation as one that defines the spread of Covid. Again, time has undoubtedly altered the judge's clumsy thinking on Covid's growing infectivity dangers.

The judge did offer to me a digital presence in the trial, but also noted that I would be *the first defendant in the state of Utah to utilize the service.* I did not then, and do not now, consider that a valid option.

Covid travels through stale air like worms tunneling through manure. Everyone in that courthouse would be at increased risk for infection and therefore, death.

I feel a certainty that with the time that has transpired and the deaths that have occurred since then, the good judge now recognizes the errors in his original thinking. Restaurants, gyms, and places of worship are the places where Covid is recognized to spread and be shared. Restaurants, gyms, and places of worship share the type of stale air that is, and will forever be, in the courtroom where the judge tried to hold my trial.

Restaurants, gyms, places of worship, and courthouses are stereotypical places of Covid contagion and death.

I'm 74 years old, and therefore at substantial risk.

When I learned of the judge's decision to hold trial during the pandemic, I was, of course, upset. I weighed the merits of going to trial in a case where the jurors have already been selected by the prosecution and come with a Big Pharma bias against ketamine, my genuinely increased likelihood of statistical death, the silent deaths of others that I knew would result from the courthouse exposures, and the likelihood that the situation might soon change. I then made the medical-legal decision to sign the stipulations while vulnerable to Covid, and then hope for changes in the near future that might alter my dilemma.

That has happened – or is about to – *with my second Moderna vaccination scheduled for the near future,* Judge Bruce Dibb will no longer have a death threat with sway to alter my thinking, and a DOPL trial will no longer threaten my life.

To summarize,

1. Dan Lau has argued for dropping the case for lack of merit.
2. Larry Gooch disallowed dropping the case for reasons that are neither medical nor legal, and that are almost certainly invalid relating to the concerns of this courtroom.
3. The stated stipulations have never been adequately discussed or shaped; they are straight from Tim Hibler, the disgraced inspector no longer working at DOPL.
4. I signed these unaltered stipulations for one reason: my life would be put at risk with the alternative.

Consider these other events of the past 4 years.

1. Tim Hibler, the initial DOPL investigator, threatened two of my nurse practitioners, telling them that their licenses would be in jeopardy if they continued at my clinic. One quit immediately, the other later. This investigator is no longer at DOPL.
2. Dr. Jeremy Kendrick, in charge of the University of Utah's ketamine clinic and therefore a direct competitor of my clinic, directed Tim Hibler in efforts to find wrong with my clinic. His primary complaint related inappropriate definitions of the concept of anesthesia. After 3 years, Tim Hibler dropped these efforts, but Dr. Kendrick continued with his conflicted interests by presenting himself as an expert witness against me. Dr. Kendrick has very obvious conflicts of interest.
3. I also view Dr. Kendrick's use of ketamine as a kind of bait-and-switch operation where he is using ketamine to attract patients to other, more monied, treatments rather than genuinely treating his patients in a quest for maximal depression relief. This type of behavior is actually an institutional misdirection that is a major theme of modern psychiatry that can be reviewed in Anne Harrington's excellent history of psychiatry, "The Mind Fixers." There is much dysfunction in the University's misuse of ketamine that is unique to the University. In short, the university has the worst ketamine response rate in the industry.
4. In an attempt to compare ketamine results, I tried 2 years ago to give a paper that I had written to Dr. Solzbacher, an associate of Dr. Kendrick at their ketamine clinic. I got no response to a written version, so I tried personal delivery. I never reached her, never saw her, but the next day I received a notice that my "assault" on Dr. Solzbacher was of such a nature that I'm never to visit the clinic again without appointment, and that I will be arrested if I do. This "assault" was a manufactured event, initiated and carried out by Tim Hibler. It was in the grotesquery of this event that I learned for the first time that this University of Utah clinic was indeed responsible for much of Tim Hibler's energies directed against me.

Why has DOPL pursued me for 4 years to address these five complaints?

1. They haven't. The complaints, which are - all but one - every day, routine complaints suffered almost daily in any ketamine clinic, are not ones to be normally prosecuted. But those minor complaints did get Tim Hibler in the door, where Dr. Kendrick's dark directives could then bring up the question of "committing anesthesia," which occupied most of Tim Hibler's conversations with me over the next three years. The anesthesia question is a fairly sophisticated one that I have addressed, I believe, quite adequately in a 19- page response to the expert witness testimony. In short, ketamine at low doses is extremely safe; in 10,000 treatments (this figure is from 6 years ago; it's now up to 98,000 treatments without a significant issue) to address the deadly disorder of depression, I've not had a single major adverse event.
2. So, the anesthesia complaint having essentially dissolved, we are left with 4 complaints which have absolutely no merit. There is a fifth event from years ago at another clinic where there was no tort and the patient had signed a special release to recognize the nature of the treatment. It suggested no risk for my current clinic.

Why did Larry Gooch really decide against dropping charges?

1. He gave no medical or legal reasons. The one he did give is simply not applicable.
2. If he does have one, shouldn't we all get to know exactly what it is? I, for one, am exceedingly curious about why the most effective depression regimen on the globe is being curtailed for, apparently, reasons of pure whimsy.
3. This is a question for which DOPL must provide a worthy answer.

Do the people of DOPL think I'm making an inappropriate killing with my admittedly busy clinic? I mean, there's gotta be some reason for all of this vacuous accusation.

1. But I'm not making money. I've not made a dime during the past 4 years of active clinic. It will, I think, now that we are beginning to contain Covid, but to date, I'm not making money.
2. If this is a primary concern, I'd be happy to make a deal: my tax returns for DOPL's dropping their harassment.
3. My goals I can display proudly. In ignoring ketamine for money and power, modern psychiatry has condemned many millions of their fellow citizens to depression and despair.
4. The goal of my ketamine clinic is very specifically to address and treat those millions of abandoned patients that formal psychiatry has condemned to lives of depression and despair.

Or is DOPL putting me and my clinic in the same category as protein supplements and other questionable treatments?

1. In Tim Hibler's words, we can see that Spravato changed what was DOPL's initial point of view here. 4 years ago, ketamine used for depression was defined as an "off-label" phenomenon; at that time, my clinic was much more vulnerable to DOPL's activity. Tim Hibler told Kelly Hooten – one of my nurse practitioners that he threatened - that, "Now that Spravato is here, we probably won't be going after Dr. Hiemstra's license."
2. The reason for this is that Spravato and ketamine are essentially the same drug; they are the same molecule, such that the off-label component is now only barely applicable to my clinic's use of ketamine. To do so – to assert that Spravato is significantly different from ketamine - *one must have special motivation.*
3. The far greater and darker truth is that Big Pharma and the disgracefully compliant industry of psychiatry are – for very monied reasons – denying their hugely suffering patients "the greatest contribution to psychiatry of the past 50 years ("Ketamine blocks bursting in the lateral habenula to rapidly relieve depression," Nature, 15 February 2018. Yan Yang.)
4. I came to this field from emergency medicine where I had been for over forty years. I came because I was disgusted by my fellow physicians denying care to the very needy in our severely depressed and anxious societies, care that IHC and

the University of Utah have decided not to give for reasons of money. I see that as unconscionable.

5. DOPL's efforts run exactly parallel to the U of U's and IHC's directives. All of these efforts are equally unconscionable.
6. I am following the general dictates of my Hippocratic oath which is, in lock step, being ignored by those choosing to contain the most societally profound drug since Thorazine.

Where are we, then? There is no reason for my being here, and I believe Dan Lau – the only man who knows – agrees with that statement.

1. Of course I, Robert Hiemstra, should be freed of this self-serving dysfunction of the past four years so that I may help to deliver the potential that is the magnificent drug ketamine to a hugely stressed society in severe need of its benefits.
2. Please remove the unwarranted public branding constituted by the stipulations printed on my license.
3. The $500 fine was a piece of calculated disgrace whose disappearance benefits everyone.
4. So that readers might understand the bigger picture of national ketamine dysfunction, **I'm including a chapter from my book, KISSD,** that explains the current role of ketamine as a threat to both Big Pharma and psychiatry as they demand to continue their money-oriented, science denying, feed-lot mode of dealing with depression, anxiety and PTSD.

End of Letter to DOPL regarding meeting of 1-21-21

Normally, Utah's Department Of Professional Licensing, DOPL, involves itself with physicians who are personally compromised or who are promoting ineffective or harmful products or procedures. These earnest personnel that generally concern themselves with corrective measures relating to wayward physicians, cannot be expected to understand that the original efforts of this case were exclusively related to the nature of anesthesia being instituted.

For 2 years Tim Hibler's only concern was about the level of anesthesia and ketamine's "off label" status. When Spravato arrived on label, Tim Hibler made the comment, "Spravato meant that we wouldn't be taking Dr. Hiemstra's license away."

And without that major directive, Tim Hibler was left without a case. That's where the prosecutor, Dan Lau, questioned the merits of the case. Without the concern of the misuse of a Schedule III drug for anesthesia, *DOPL is now left to pursue complaints of no valid medical merit.*

And without medical merit, the Department Of Professional Licensing must rely for its sense of validity and decency upon the death threats from an ill-informed judge.

And a final note to underline the hostility of the 1-21-21 probation meeting.

DOPL probation requires what the organization calls a "Supervisor" to oversee the compromised physician as he conducts his medical duties. The physician is responsible for finding his own supervisor.

After my UMIA attorney, Greg Soderberg, failed over the course of 3-4 months to find a physician willing to fill that role, I thought that I had found a psychiatrist who could fill the role.

This psychiatrist-as-DOPL-supervisor only lasted for a few weeks, though, because his office staff, "Made me quit, threatening to quit if I continued my relationship with Dr. Hiemstra." He has, indeed, quit.

I can't know the intimate motivations of the psychiatrist's office staff, but the psychiatrist said that it was raw fear of DOPL. They are concerned that the psychiatrist will offer a medical opinion that will conflict with that of DOPL, thereby bringing about a DOPL backlash that will hurt the psychiatrist and his office and staff. They – two of them - are standing by their promise to quit if he offers his services as a DOPL supervisor.

This supervisor is important to the life of my medical license and clinic. Simultaneously requiring a supervisor while playing a role in sabotaging him – however unintentional – ought to conjure some level of responsibility.

The coming days ought to be ones of revelation, though DOPL's motivations seem to be growing ever darker with their clarity.

CHAPTER 8

Robert C. Hiemstra's Grievances Against DOPL

They are trying to steal the best of my dreams and
believe themselves to have succeeded.

I practiced emergency medicine for forty years, much of it in the toughest malpractice state in America – California – and never suffered a lawsuit or major complaint. Then I came to Utah as ketamine was making its multiply obstructed entrance onto the American scene. I came to Utah for emergency medicine but was immediately enamored with the potential of ketamine in a world where everyone knew that psychiatry's SSRIs were worse than worthless when compared to this old anesthetic that had suddenly become our newest and most promising antidepressant.

I came to Utah and found the best and most rewarding medical dreams of my life. I really did, for the first time in my life, become a healer with a star to follow. I was a medical man on a mission with a message of healing, love and happiness. There are few paths available to human beings where the goals are truly focused on the welfare of the society as a whole. Most star-enchanted journeys are self-absorbed things involving money, power and glamour. The true healer may find himself tagged with these attributes, but they are secondary – follow- ons to the primary motivation.

I didn't come to Utah to confront psychiatry and Big Pharma on a national stage, but that stage is the only field on which this game can be played. Now that I'm here, I've been given no choice. Either I fight back against these predators or literally millions of sufferers will continue to suffer the disease that most specifically acts to destroy that which makes us most human: our dynamic creativity directing an irrepressible need for self-expression.

But I came to a Utah that was recoiling from the shocks suffered at the height of the opiate crisis, which many consider to be the greatest social and medical disruption since the Civil War. During this cataclysm Utah was ranked 8th worst in the country – and this was Mormon country no less, with a unique style of spiritual expression developed during a century and a half in the American wild west followed by the sequential summing of tens of thousands of individual, family, stake, and general cultural losses to opiates – so that when I showed up on the scene presenting a psychedelic that promised to save them and to do so safely, they became furiously incredulous and resistive.

During all of this time I have presented only the science, and promised simply the numbers - the drug efficacies where ketamine could relieve their depression 70% of the time and do it safely.

I didn't even try to assert ketamine's ability to deal with opiate addiction, which is a stealth ketamine superpower. And know that once ketamine is finally utilized for opiate rehabilitation, this openly disparaged drug could serve to rehabilitate psychiatry and Big Pharma themselves where they could then repair much of the dent-that-is-addiction in the use of conventional opiates that they are—and will always be—responsible for.

So, the opiate-furious citizens of Utah—harassed by years of those opiates written for by their own physicians but, at the same time, unable to discern that this particular psychedelic that was ketamine was actually an important part of the answer to the opiate problem rather than being a fellow demon of the illicit drug world—these furious Utah citizens mistook ketamine for oxycodone and dealt me blow after hurtful blow.

And I've felt every one of them, however inappropriate they might have been.

Whether DOPL (Utah's Department of Professional Licensing), Dr. Kendrick or Dr. Salzbarger at the university, Judge Dibb pushing Covid-filled trials, or my own attorney, Greg Soderberg having served previously as a DOPL judge - they have allowed the assistant attorney general, Dan Lau, to construct his dark and artful mechanism of eternal probation as I twist slowly in a foul wind redolent of their corruption. His plans—I've been told from the inside by respectable authority—are and have always been intended to simply keep me here forever, sort of a Napoleon-on-Elba (probably without the arsenic) kind of thing.

Know that when I use the word "everyone" here, I mean it. I can add up to 3 billion souls across the globe (there are only 10 billion total) that have been determined to be in need of ketamine with its unique effectiveness for their depression, anxiety and PTSD. Now, I know and obsess over this monumental fact, but at the very moment of my emergence onto the Utah scene, the dysfunctional in our profession conspired on multiple fronts to take me down with the help of the opiate crisis. Is this a RICO situation? It certainly has all the fingers.

So, the complex picture that I'm trying to paint is of medically-innocent-and-scheduled-to-be-fruitful-with-ketamine me bursting onto a dark and furious scene of widespread and culturally diffuse opiate abuse that provided an "overstory" as painted by Malcom Gladwell that then pressed a Utah backstory that struggled to construct a frustrated and inappropriate prosecution of me.

That's my story and I believe it to be irrevocably and invitingly true as I twist slowly here in the breeze without a medical license that I can use or get to.

Ketamine also has great-but-unexplored potential for opiate rehabilitation that relates to the portion of its pharmaceutical pedigree that is opiate. This will be explored during the next decades, but its opiate-fighting attributes are available now. While in this area of high- tower mental health criticism, let me comment on the University of Utah's Mental Health Service's corrupt offering to the opiate-troubled people of Utah.

I say assertively and accusingly that the ketamine clinic ("Failed Depression Clinic") at the university is not what it seems. They may have ketamine up there, but it's all bait and switch from what I can see. They want to get you up there and then switch you to something more remunerative. That's why they're open only two afternoons a week and that's why they use minimalist ketamine doses that are not constructed with success in mind.

And know that I believe that psychiatry's current efforts to thwart the use and expansion of conventional ketamine – if effective in diminishing ketamine availability – would continue to expand their patients' suffering as well as the general societal dysfunction around them. Please pay attention to this most gripping and revealing part of the story as I deliver parts of Malcom Gladwell's great new book, *Revenge of the Tipping point,* as he discusses many surprising-as- unfathomable twists that distort our futures toward dark forests and cold seas populated by unknowable intelligences.

Know that I believe Purdue Pharmaceutical's general opiate dysfunction to have extended long ago to our culture here in Utah to include the people of DOPL as well as the rest of the mental health community. This social alteration of local truth – Mr. Gladwell refers to it as "overstory" – would have occurred in a manner similar to that described in the book just mentioned where it spends its time making the case that the Purdue opiate overstory was free to inflict its damage onto every red state society of the nation owing to the lack of prescription controls for opiates.

This opiates-run-amuck situation did not occur with the same abandon in blue states owing to the deceptive effectiveness of California's triplicate prescriptions which then made their "bookkeeper's delight" way to every state that Malcolm defined as blue. The states utilizing opiate triplicates could, then, keep track of every single pill as it first originated at a physician's pen and pad where the physician kept one of the three prescription copies and gave two to the patient.

The patient then took those two to the pharmacy where the pharmacy filled the prescription for the patient, kept one copy, and sent the other to the state *where an address and a name will sit forever beside a record of every pill ever prescribed in the state.*

But if that prescription was written in a red state—like #8 opiate society in America, Utah—every doctor can be a state-protected opiate super spreader. Utah keeps its professional pushers safe, or at least it did so for decades.

Now, whether or not these triplicates can account for our politics as Mr. Gladwell very effectively suggests in the book, I cannot say, but that there has been societal disruption, confusion, and general hostility at the societal level from these opiates, my entire time in Utah has seemed to reflect that truth in a seemingly fundamental chaos.

At this moment, the medical authorities in Utah have effectively taken my medical license by hanging it on a hook of "probation" where the esoteric rules of that hook define the license as unusable. And these furious-as-dysfunctional zealots have determined that I cannot practice medicine in Utah or any other state owing to interstate reciprocities that Utah has imposed to underline its will.

This means that:

> Though I formally have a license and pay to keep it current, I'm not effectively a doctor and cannot practice medicine.

I'm not allowed to work to make money as a doctor and I cannot publicly present myself as a physician.

This means that I must hire practitioners to fill the physician role in my clinic, which requires money from me that I do not readily have. This threatens the mental health of over 4800 patients that would not have access to the unique process, KISSD, if the clinic did not exist.

My new and evolving depression clinic's (Ketamine for Depression Salt Lake City) very existence has been—and is being—threatened by my personally being unable to provide the full financial practicalities of a medical clinic that I would have available if my license were intact.

I cannot currently afford medical conferences or continuing education while in this induced state of poverty.

FHTA and Medicare are both calling about supplements for housing and food, and I need them.

Patients that are sick will be left to suffer. This apex source of depression care is being threatened, and the 4800 patients currently receiving care that is not available at any other facility may be forced to reenter the world of depression that ketamine has freed them from.

Further, the KISSD: Ketamine Intramuscular Stepped System for Depression process is as unique as it is effective. No other medical process can currently offer the 100 days of freedom from depression that KISSD offers to 70% of patients treated with the process. This means that, because no other medical entity offers this level of efficacy, this threat to KISSD that would be local for any lesser medicine, should be extended to the 400 million depression sufferers worldwide as well as the 2 billion more estimated to suffer from anxiety. And we still haven't counted those suffering PTSD, probably another 400 million worldwide.

Specifically, as the scientists that we at least pretend to be, medicine usage should be determined by its statistical efficacy in comparison to other medicines being

> considered. As such, we know that Prozac and its fellows have an antidepressant power determined to be "17% of a placebo," which does not produce enough of an effect to be recognized by either the patient or the examiner outside of the clinical setting. This "single bite of a flea" minimalism pales to non-existence when compared to KISSD's 100 days of freedom from depression. And know that this huge discrepancy in treatment—as you go from the "17% of a sugar pill that is Prozac," to the 100 days of depression freedom that is the "Holy Grail of Depression that is KISSD"— is both massive and exactly what this scientific discussion is supposed to be about.
>
> And please know that I have a patent pending on the KISSD process that could very well allow me and KISSD to utilize unique access to the rest of the planet. And further— as if you hadn't noticed— know that the planet is in turmoil and is looking for the extreme relief and direction that KISSD promises.
>
> And finally, know that my Hippocratic Oath demands that I not only struggle to bring this supreme instance of healing to a planet that is screaming from its ten thousand times ten thousand wounds, but that that oath demands that I demand that the hypocrites of their Hippocratic Oaths cease and desist in their active and heartless suppression of ketamine for monetary gain. With this view of healing, the specialty of psychiatry deserves a reclassification to a status of renegade criminal element, a thorough public spanking, and a redirection with tools of both psychiatry and our criminal justice system.

So, if I call myself innocent of all these charges, where did all of this accusation come from? As I mentioned earlier, in Malcolm Gladwell's recent book, *Revenge of the Tippingpoint,* he makes the startling point that the red state – blue state political divide correlates convincingly with the use of triplicate prescription writing for opiates. He suggests that the widespread societal decay - witnessed in rural areas in particular and red state societies more generally - is a product of the corruption and dysfunction that follow multiple pathways in Gladwell's "overstory" portrait of both legal and illegal run-amuck opiate distribution. He goes further in a very sophisticated argument to suggest that this opiate corruption explains our current red state-blue state politics. Whether or not that explanation is valid for politics, there is no question that oxycodone and oxycontin abuse originating at the highest levels of society have created massive problems at all levels of our culture.

Blue states suffered, too, but much less initially owing to the prescription triplicates (though Hawaii utilizes an electronic records control system that is touted to be equally effective) that give authorities the ability to identify the perpetrators early before the opiate distribution networks are up and running.

Whereas the states that did implement California's triplicate prescriptions for opiate control experienced little immediate opiate-related societal disruption or rise in the suicide rate, states that did not control their opiates were devasted and continue to suffer even now. Gladwell quotes compelling figures comparing his blue states with triplicates to red states without. Though his red-blue breakdown doesn't correspond exactly with current politics (Texas gets to be a blue state by Malcolm's reckoning), the divide has major consequences. Consider this list of figures defining effects on our society that he attributes to opiate consequence in general and the release of OxyContin and OxyContin Pro in particular:

1. Opiate deaths immediately jumped in non-triplicate states to stay elevated for 20 years.
2. Economic growth and workforce participation has been consistently stronger in triplicate states.
3. Health outcomes of babies fared better, and child neglect was lower in triplicate states.
4. At the time of the introduction of OxyContin, red states experienced an actual rise in property crimes of 12% and violent crimes of 25% compared to blue states. These figures for crime are counted as "unheard of" by the professional gathering the numbers: "Honestly," said Sim, the economist, "when I first got this result, I didn't really believe the result myself."

As a red state, Utah has suffered much. Utah ranked #8 on the list of states that socially embraced oxycodone and oxycontin as the general depression, family dysfunction, and suicide rates skyrocketed. Of course this fundamentalist Mormon state could have been predicted to have mounted a furious response to this moral, physical, social, and spiritual threat - and it did.

Into this fury I walked in 2017, knowing that ketamine was the validly-described super medicine for depression that no other drug had ever been, and that I - as an emergency medicine physician - could appropriately manage the ketamine anesthesia that the drug was designed to produce. After all, I had been trained specifically for this type of medical procedure, where a psychiatrist hadn't professionally seen an orifice below the belt since her internship.

I stand proudly as a qualified ERMD of particularly defining skills as I say that, and I will professionally look down on any conventional psychiatrist who suggests that he is professionally capable of administering ketamine.

We may assume that I've made my point on the conventional lack of comparable skills when comparing a psychiatrist to a professional capable of safely administering an anesthetic agent and monitoring the response.

So, expecting to be welcomed with open arms by a psychiatry that was educationally, experientially, and avariciously opposed to this psychedelic medicine that could effectively treat many of their depression patients, I was as surprised as professionally horrified by their multiple, conflicted positions. After all, as I just mentioned, psychiatrists never bother to acquire the monitoring skills required for a medicine of this type. Pills, electroshock, talk therapy, and maybe TMS define the full spectrum of treatment available to psychiatry for medically addressing depression.

Where ketamine is utilized at the University of Utah, it is limited to a stunted version of minimum effectiveness where it is simply not allowed to compete against more remunerative tools such as pills or electroshock therapy. Additionally, the drug as presented in the university's setting has been defined as requiring an anesthesiologist for its administration; the psychiatrist managing the case is not qualified for the monitoring of anesthesia. And this clinic at the U of U is a particularly suspect case in that it is open only two afternoons a week and, when they finally are given, the ketamine doses are extremely minimal in a drug that specifically benefits with higher dosing.

And we must not forget that the hazards of insufficient treatment for depression include both more depression as well as suicide.

It is my belief that the University of Utah's failed depression clinic is not meant to truly address depression. Their reason for this is not clear. I would guess that they are either "bait-and-switching" with the ketamine to get the patients to their other more remunerative tools, or they are simply cripplingly timid in their efforts to treat the worst disease known to man.

The answer to that question lies within the frontal lobes of the university psychiatrist of that clinic, Dr. Kendrick. He is the doctor that looked across town to see my clinic – the busiest and "healingest" depression clinic in the country, if not the world – and directed newly appointed DOPL officer Tim Hibler at me. He had nothing, this ex-traffic cop, but he persisted for two years to ask questions of anesthesia from Dr. Kendrick that he never understood (and that psychiatrist Dr. Kendrick didn't understand either), and finally took me to trial with little merit and a lot of hope.

But the trial was scheduled to take place during the Covid pandemic where we were all witnesses to medical fact often mattering less than political allegiance. My first trial was postponed, but in the second trial the judge demanded that we proceed (I was told that murder trials were being postponed while my trial had to go on) and announced that he—the judge that would be constructing aerosols immediately in front of us all in that still courthouse—would not be wearing a mask during the trial.

I'm 78 years old and was 76 years old then and made medical decisions for myself that were in part a product of other's hostile politics. I still stand by those decisions, but I would have preferred not to have made them, to have had a trial and an exchange of ideas. A reasonable, non-infectious trial would certainly have been preferable, especially knowing now the potential lethality of a Covid judge's deep and aerosol-manufacturing voice, as well as the now-obvious fact of the emergence of the Alpha variant at that time, which was 43 times more infectious.

And, of course, if I had known of DOPL's intention to artificially hamstring my license, I might have acted differently. But I think those plans for my license had been laid down before the trial as this man has apparently done many times in a past described as repeatedly scandalous.

Looking back, the trial and everything before it had a feeling of being scheduled. There was no question at that time about what the outcome of the trial would be; both I and people at every level knew that I was to be put on probation. Even my attorney felt that probation was unavoidable. And this inevitable ending was coming despite the total lack of merit.

When I brought up taking the trial to Drs. Kendrick and Salzbarger by linking their motivations with that of Investigator Hibler, my attorney assigned to me, Greg Soderberg, informed me that the allotted

$25,000 would be inadequate to pursue that truth, even though he never explained to me what laws were broken or who was harmed. This man—the assigned counselor from my malpractice carrier now informing me of my inadequate funds at this late date—was, he told me along the way, previously a DOPL judge.

With probation a perceived near-certainty, when presented with my coming trial during the apex of the COVID pandemic—the only trial that wasn't postponed for COVID concerns in Utah, including murder trials—I calculated that many COVID deaths (not to mention my own at age 76) that would statistically occur if the trial took place, would simply not occur if the trial were cancelled. So, with fewer likely calculated deaths—deaths that might include my own—but with no likely change in legal outcome, I pled guilty.

The original points of accusation – what DOPL terms "stipulations" – were not related to any genuine legal concerns or broken laws (I learned this later from DOPL people on the inside who were also too frightened of DOPL to consider representing me). Those stipulations were simply not meritorious.

My anonymous DOPL counselor related how there was apparently a gathering where a social moment of "lightheartedness and laughter" took place. During this bubbly moment Assistant Attorney General Dan Lau "cut and pasted the meaningless stipulations" onto my nationally published record, which would turn out to be effectively the final summary of my career if my medical license was to be as crippled and dead-ended as Dan Lau wished it to be.

"Meaningless" the woman had said. "Meaningless," she said as my medical license was proxy-shredded into small bits to be viewed by a contemptuous public as spoiled moments in a physician's fouled life. Dan Lau laughed with others as he cut up and tried to disgrace a life that was so very much more filled with healing and a fundamental goodness that was itself so much greater and fulfilled than any thought that his disgraceful and petty mind could ever imagine.

If the man had simply delivered a sentence, I could try to relax. But this particularly sadistic relish taken at the expense of my lifetime of goodness and great effort so thoroughly trashed by evil is not to be forgotten.

Will it be revenge? This is much more than simple revenge.

In short, I don't believe that there is a shred of legal validity in those posted stipulations. And I have been hugely wronged. But more importantly, medicine itself has been wronged. And along with medicine, our society and—for God's sake—Dr. Kendrick and Dan Lau have hurt themselves and our professions with this trash.

And that last paragraph's list of wronged entities leaves out the most harmed, which are the patients themselves that include the 40 million, the 2 billion, the 3 billion – or however many there are that could be—but won't be—made healthy and happy or at least better – if ketamine were to be as suppressed as Big Pharma and psychiatry hope it to be.

Making this situation right truly makes the world a much better place.

No suits in 40 years.

This all comes from a crass and venal business man across town and a skankily malicious Assistant Attorney General with a Jabba-the- Hut taste for stipulations.

And while in this induced state of poverty, I have creditors knocking as the FHTA is trying to offer me assisted housing.

I can't afford conferences or Con-ed.

The pure morality of defending me is immense, but my accusers— here in Mormon Salt Lake City—presume a default position of morality by virtue of propinquity to the temple, a universally understood local phenomenon. Downstream healing has huge promise if I'm freed. This blend of creepy, self-absorbed, hurtful-to-others power that is being used to stop my incredible march of healing is remarkable at both ends of the observation.

The wrongs committed here occur at multiple levels, over different time periods, and as consequences of forces and influences far removed from any of the accusations actually levelled against Hiemstra as well as the criminalities committed while in wild pursuit of him at other's request.

The wrongs are multiple, unrelated to original stipulations, widespread over many people, have both medical as well as simply cheesy business origins, but these wrongs have exceedingly negative effects at local, city, state, national and global levels.

I signed those stipulations believing that to be the safest, least-deadly path out of a Covid-filled courtroom intentionally and medically misunderstood by the judge presiding over it. That courtroom at the height of the pandemic was a COVID incubator for me, the attorneys, the judge, and every member of that courthouse staff who stayed home as a result of my trial having been cancelled; I am statistically certain lives were saved as a result of that courthouse remaining closed. Science did not understand at that time the deadly effectiveness of viral aerosolization in keeping every infectious particle suspended on mucus microdroplets for many hours at a coughing. Judges with deep and loud voices would likely become, indeed, particularly pernicious varieties of great superspreaders during the pandemic, first corralling victims into the courthouse, and then "talking the virus at everyone."

Though the prosecution was initiated and performed by, of course, prosecutors, this was a conflict over quite sophisticated medical topics that were really beyond the attorneys present. In fact, on the subject least understood by Tim Hibler, the DOPL investigator—anesthesia—the physician least knowledgeable but most emotionally motivated to pursue my prosecution, Dr. Kendrick, was a psychiatrist with *no formal training in anesthesia.*

And know that this all took place with the knowledge, OK, participation, and almost certainly the encouragement of the University proper. Isn't DOPL and the U of U of a piece? I certainly thought so with the loose restraining orders flying around, and the assertions of "No merit," from the likes of Larry Gooch.

I wish that I could simply walk into a university auditorium and say to every health practioner in Utah, "Hello, I'm Robert Hiemstra offering you the uniquely effective treatment KISSD: Ketamine Intramuscular Stepped System for Depression. You will see transformations that have never occurred before its creation back during the sixties.

But we are being hampered by a dysfunctional psychiatry and a Big Pharma that is as predacious as any robber baron, and equally as heartless.

The process is patent pending with an answer promised soon. DOPL managed to bear-trap my medical license with the strangest of Judge Dibb-wielded clueless crowbars applied at the height of the pandemic.

These past seven years have been the most exciting, consequential and medically fruitful days of my medical life. And with psychiatry's curious and seemingly moneyed reluctance to embrace ketamine I've become somewhat righteous in what I regard as my Hippocratic contempt for Big Pharma and psychiatry as they continue to try to do to SSRIs what they tried to do to insulin a few years ago. Now, Matt Dillon wouldn't have liked what psychiatry is doing to the people under their medical care, so excuse me if I choose to ride with Matt Dillon, even though I know that they're going to want to rip his beating heart from his chest like they were fevered Aztecs. Or at least to continue to withhold my medical license.

And shouldn't that Sword of Happiness have a name? Of course it should.

And shouldn't DOPL and Dr. Kendrick and my phony attorney Greg Soderberg, not to mention Judge Dibb, all pay some $5 million or

$50 or $500 million.

And is this a RICO-type structure, whether fed or state?

How many people will remain depressed as a consequence of my license being suppressed? Well, if I'm the one to deliver the mental health goods to the planet, the citizens rejoicing could number in the tens or hundreds of millions of happy patients relieved of their depression.

If so, what depression Big Pharma cultivates by allowing, I treat. Big Pharma-Psychiatry inflicts the disease and suffering that I cure.

And now we've reached our apex feature in this sordid tale of worst of Pharoah-level afflictions.

We all recognize the pain and suffering that comes with poverty. We all recognize the humiliations of demotion, especially when its so sudden, so unwarranted, and so total (but maliciously-as-calculatedly pretending otherwise). And this demotion is from such altitude; I'm a proudly competent ERMD in a spotless white coat, and I have always deserved that coat. And I have just developed THE MOST EFFICACIOUS TREATMENT FOR DEPRESSION ON THE PLANET.

And that as I was progressively forced to define myself against the assaults of psychiatry, I see a growing role for that Matt Dillon portion of my personality that must protect the depressed settlers from the cattle rustlers that constitute modern psychiatry. And to know that it was those same cattle-rustling psychiatrists that have delivered the blow that is beyond criminal insanity as it spiritually transgresses any healer's fundamental admonition against harming those under one's care. Especially when your Hippocratic violation is so crassly motivated by money. Is psychiatry truly a renegade criminal element as its approach to both SSRIs and insulin suggest?

Their Hippocratic Oaths—those psychiatrists—are here being systematically violated; from Hippocrat to hypocrite they fall with the ease and clink of a coin.

CHAPTER 9

Elon Musk and a Terrible Circularity of Ketamine

Elon Musk and the Terrible Circularity of Ketamine: A Reflection on Depression, Power, and the Future of 200 Million Americans

By Robert Hiemstra, M.D.

Introduction: A Mind of Monumental Influence

Elon Musk is not just another billionaire with a few rockets and some self-driving cars. He is the wealthiest man in the world, commander of SpaceX, Tesla, X (formerly Twitter), and an ever-expanding empire that bridges everything from electric vehicles to underground tunnels and brain-computer interfaces. But behind the polished aluminum panels and stock surges lies a man grappling with what seems to be significant and persistent depression.

Reports, both first-hand and speculative, have identified Musk's use of ketamine as a means of treatment. Though the exact nature of his regimen remains undisclosed, it is clear from public behavior and admissions that he is engaging in what some might call 'unconventional approaches'—which may, on occasion, resemble a party more than a prescription pad.

It is within this context that we must begin a critical, respectful, and genuinely concerned analysis of Musk's influence on the 200 million Americans who depend on Social Security, Medicare, Medicaid, and the Veteran's Administration. Because, believe it or not, Musk's mental health may well be one of the most important public health and policy matters of our time.

The Loop of Terrible Circularity

Let us trace the loop:

1. Elon Musk, suffering from some measure of bipolar depression, receives ketamine treatment.
2. These treatments, and the renewed vitality they may grant, propel his work across ventures funded in large part by public tax dollars—billions from the American government.
3. Emboldened, or perhaps chemically loosened, Musk aligns himself with the MAGA movement and engages in high-visibility political activism.
4. His political influence now aims at dismantling the very systems—Social Security, Medicare, Medicaid, and the VA—that supported his rise through their contributions, contracts, and tax-funded innovation incentives.
5. Should this dismantling succeed, those same citizens—our aging, our veterans, our sick, our most vulnerable—will fall into a new wave of anxiety, despair, and depression.
6. And what will they be prescribed and administered? You guessed it. Ketamine.

We've gone from Musk's depression to a nationwide ketamine boom that closes the circle—a Terrible Circularity, as I call it—with tragic symmetry.

The MAGAfication of Elon: Is It Politics or Psychedelics?

This is a delicate but essential question: Is the personality shift we are witnessing in Mr. Musk—his insensitive commentary, his alliances with political radicals, his assault on the financial safety net—primarily the result of political ideology or psychedelic side effects?

Of course, many MAGA adherents share a penchant for outlandish rhetoric and disdain for traditional institutions. But Musk adds another layer: a documented flirtation with ketamine, a drug known to disinhibit, intensify, and sometimes confuse emotional responses. The result? He speaks of dismantling the foundational support systems of American life with the casual tone of someone choosing toppings for a pizza.

If ketamine is the cause—or even a contributor—then we're in new territory. We are witnessing, potentially, the first mass-distribution societal side effect of an improperly monitored psychedelic treatment. This is less a medical malpractice case and more a civilizational one.

The Unprecedented Reach of One Man's Mood

Normally, one man's depression wouldn't matter much outside his home or, at most, his boardroom. But Musk is not a normal man, and this is not a normal situation. With influence across defense, transportation, social media, artificial intelligence, and cryptocurrency, Musk's decisions ripple across global economies and national policies.

And when he proposes to gut the financial backbone of 200 million Americans, the question becomes more than personal—it becomes national, even existential. It's no longer "Is Elon okay?" It's "Are **we** okay, and what the hell is happening to our social fabric?"

Sayla Love and the Atlantic: The Case of a Misleading Headline

In her Atlantic article titled, "What Ketamine Does to the Human Brain," Sayla Love attempted a delicate dance between science, social commentary, and celebrity medicine. But given its laser focus on Elon Musk's behavior, it may have been more appropriately titled, "What Is Ketamine Really Doing to Elon's Brain?"

While not devoid of scientific insight, the article largely highlights the voyeuristic fascination with Musk's condition and its unpredictable effect on global systems. It blurs the line between a personal medical narrative and a collective societal threat.

The result is a strange sort of intimacy with Elon—one we didn't ask for but now must endure.

The Closing of the Loop: Depression to Depression

As Musk's policies unfold, and if indeed they lead to the collapse of Social Security, Medicare, and other vital institutions, tens of millions will descend into mental health crises. The irony is brutal and complete: the very drug Musk used for relief will become the national balm for the wounds he helped inflict.

This is not poetic justice. It is just tragedy. With extra steps.

From a Puppy's Trauma to Human Fragility

Let me offer something personal. Last week, I nearly killed my puppy Bronco with a mis-thrown stick. Watching his tiny body go limp after a seizure broke something inside me. I cried. Not tough-guy, movie-crying. Real, ragged sobbing—the kind I never knew I was capable of. In that moment, I understood something profound about mood, emotion, trauma, and the unpredictability of our nervous systems.

We are fragile. Our feelings are not programmable. Our decisions—no matter how powerful we are—emerge from forces inside us that we don't fully understand. That's as true for a ketamine-treated billionaire as it is for a sobbing middle-aged man cradling his dog in the grass, or our 200 million fellow citizens staring up at the chainsaw at this moment.

Homeostasis, Valence, and the Role of the Human Organ

In the field of neuroscience, homeostasis refers to the body's ability to maintain internal stability. Valence is the emotional weight of a stimulus—what draws us toward or pushes us away.

These concepts govern not just moods, but cultures. They shape our voting, our wars, our alliances. And sometimes, they help men like Elon Musk rise to Olympian heights, then act out their inner chaos on the world stage. As the old joke goes about which organ should rule the body—the brain, the heart, or the anus—we know who usually wins: the one that can stop everything by simply refusing to move.

And so, we find ourselves here—watching the richest man in the world use chainsaws as metaphors, social security as a Ponzi scheme, and ketamine as a coping mechanism. And we ask: can this be sustainable? Can this be safe?

Conclusion: Inter-Subjective Realities and the Ethics of Power

Yuval Harari coined the term "inter-subjective reality" to describe the shared fictions that bind us—money, nations, religion. Musk, through his depression and his treatment, is rewriting parts of this shared fiction.

This makes it imperative—not optional—that his doctors, his investors, and perhaps even his fellow citizens engage more seriously with the medical and ethical ramifications of his mental state.

Because when 200 million Americans are one executive decision away from despair, that's not just a mental health issue. That's a national emergency.

And if ketamine got us into this loop, it had better not be the only tool we've got to get out of it.

CHAPTER 10

The Corporatization of Bob

To be free each of us needs the truth, but factuality requires institutions as well as risk-takers. If freedom is the value of life, one of its forms is the self-conscious labor of making freedom possible for others.

ON Freedom, Timothy Snyder, Crown New York 2024

DOPL's letter of June 5th of this year makes much of four assertions of "unprofessional conduct," which is defined generally as violating the terms of an order governing a license. These entities are securing a supervisor, submitting a practice plan, finishing the required continuing education, and being present at our last communication.

All of this focuses on the events following my dealing with Judge Dibb, and DOPL's assertions studiously focus on anything but the actual reasons for my being here, which are both complicated and free of significant wrongdoing on my part. In fact, I will make the case that inappropriate accusation came initially only from the University's Dr. Kendrick; DOPL only entered into impropriety when its "dark force" chose to utilize the "supervisor leave'em hangin'" tool where the actual unprofessional conduct of DOPL evolves to full-fledged fraud. I will deal with the four instances of supposed misconduct one by one, but first the landscape must be clarified with foundational truths.

Inconvenient Truths:

1. I have never been tried or prosecuted for a single infraction.
2. The accusations made against me at the time the trial was decided upon had absolutely no merit and no tort has ever been suggested.
3. I was put into a medicolegal, decision-making situation where I knew from multiple conversations with my attorney and others that my legal fate had already been determined by the extra-constitutional system that is DOPL.

4. I then signed those stipulations for health reasons – both mine and the public's health – that were more related to the dangers of the epidemic than to the specious, compromised legalisms presented as stipulations by Dan Lau, the head attorney. Then, Judge Dibb's carnival-like mask threat dutifully echoed MAGA's contrary Covid positioning that he then twisted to manipulate the legal proceedings from the bench.
5. When Judge Dibb announced that he would not wear a Covid mask, it came at a moment where I recognized the courthouse was going to be kept open for my trial alone (all other trials in the state of Utah but mine—from murder to traffic violation— had already been postponed.) Knowing that I was on a scheduled track for being voted guilty for some specious variety of DOPL restriction that simply had no merit, I made a decision that I viewed as consistent with my Hippocratic Oath and common decency. I'm not sure now that it was tactically the right one (who would have guessed at the judge's departure from propriety,) but it was guided by honor and the science of medicine and statistically was very likely to have saved lives. I hadn't planned on the "supervisor leave'em-hangin'" tool at that time.
6. Also, the "medical reasoning" of the court's situation has since been clarified; Covid does indeed transmit primarily by aerosol, such that a single superspreader in Judge Dibb's position (the judge himself) would have filled up the entire courthouse with his Covid-infected mucous after only two or three throaty expulsions. I was, therefore, medically correct; Judge Dibb owes me a personal thanks for having prevented him from unknowingly killing a number of his fellow citizens.
7. Listed last here—but probably the greatest of these truths— is that of my having developed a treatment for depression that is many times more effective than the current offerings of psychiatry. Guided by jealous neighbors (Dr. Kendrick at the university was the greatest medical offender, seeking prosecution of rivals rather than simply providing good medicine), their venom is what initially prompted Tim Hibler, the initial DOPL investigator, to become ferociously illegal and pursue me without valid merit.

8. It was right here, sir—with Tim Hibler nosing Dr. Kendrick over and over again—that the unprofessional conduct both began and persisted for years.

The Unprofessional Conduct broken down.

Really, all four (minus number four, which is only about being late) will be addressed with the supervisor issue, which becomes here in Utah much more than a tool of supervision of the physician and more a tool of containment, control, dissolution and death of a license. Let us begin.

In California this situation of mine would have resulted in a supervisor previously trained by the court. This person would then be assigned to a given doctor to provide oversight both to the doctor and to the court. The California program then proceeds very much as was initially described for Utah with payments made by the offending physician to the supervising physician to cover his time. The process is awkward, foreign to everyone, downright weird and—when coupled to asking a physician to add a strange activity to his already busy load—it is quite off-putting, at least the Utah version.

From a distance - way out here in Utah - I would say that California's system probably got the balance right.

I would liken Utah's mandatory courtship of the supervisor to having to ask a public bus driver busy at his job to stop the bus and change your kid's diapers while she's working; even paying her doesn't make it right. This particular portion of DOPL's supervisor requirement has all the earmarks of having been designed with fraud in mind.

But even with the courtship requirement, I actually did find a doctor, a psychiatrist, who was initially quite excited about helping me. We had earlier shared a patient, a depressed and suicidal veteran. This psychiatrist was well-versed on the effectiveness of ketamine. Everything seemed fine for about a month. Then, finally, one dark morning he called to tell me that he could not perform the service.

The reason he gave was that his staff had rebelled at the thought that he would try to help another physician that DOPL was restricting. These mental health nurses were incensed by his altruism and asserted that they would quit his practice, every one of them, and leave him alone.

That's what mental health nurses do when their psychiatrist moves to help another physician.

I, of course, found that hugely unlikely, unreasonable, and a situation that brought to the fore all of the stories I'd heard about the over-flexed power and general sway of DOPL. Fear of a particularly nasty sort seems to be a general tool fiercely available to DOPL as perceived by the community. Physicians have told me things like, "You've gotta be careful with these guys… I always slide on the white coat when I hear that a DOPL guy is coming over."

This was post-trial, so I had had literally years to gather stories of DOPL. The psychiatrist was deeply apologetic, and I could see the pain.

The staff story being thoroughly questionable, I assumed then that a whispered few dark words from DOPL had carried enough motivation to paralyze this psychiatrist to his current pained inaction.

I remember wondering at the time of the intonation of such a threat. I mean, I've never really heard one outside of a movie. How would it be made to this very sophisticated guy? Would I ever find out?

Lucky insight was charging my way on a great dark horse, but for a few more months I continued to ask more doctors if they would perform the task; I, of course, found no one.

A number of times I dialed DOPL informally to ask again about their helping me find someone, but again and again they had nothing to say or suggest.

They apparently did not note my calls, at least as suggested by the simple and bare and somewhat incomplete complaint: "provided no supervisor."

As I became more and more frustrated and as I came to realize with ever greater certainty that I was lost in a prescribed maze (no triplicate prescriptions here) that had been constructed with cold intention, I considered a lawsuit in this land that is so famous for its extreme medico-legal regulation. Never having experienced this world before—California, after all, is the land of law and all that is legal—I still had hopes of finding balance again.

So, I found a lawyer that lifted the lids of both eyes so that a vision exploded before me. It is a sad and sordid thing—this vision—that is here at this moment revealing a piece of truth with the writing of these words.

To this attorney who has opened my eyes, I extend huge credibility. She presents herself as a coddled DOPL insider who has worked the ropes of the organization for years.

(Both she and the other dark entity she will be describing shall remain unnamed, though I'm sure insiders will have no problem identifying either of them.)

She works as a DOPL attorney apparently filling specific roles and needs as they appear. "I have lunch with them every day," she told us.

I told her right away that I was looking for an aggressive lawyer to defend me in some type of action against DOPL.

She made immediately clear that, "My job would be over if I defended you."

But she went on to make the point that for her to take on clients specifically under siege by DOPL could also be dangerous. Her tone changed as her eyes widened. She was nervous, but it was obvious that she wanted to be taken seriously.

"He does things," she said with wide eyes. "Bad things. I mean, like, real murder. I've seen it."

In the room at that time there were two other people. My clinic partner was one, and the friend who had brought in this lady attorney was the other. She had, of course, all of our attention.

What was this lady saying, really? I had little clue, but I do remember wondering if I had a legal responsibility of some kind to report this. In medicine we have a Hippocratic Oath that suggests this sort of responsibility but the oath is not law, even though certain aspects, such as reporting medical misconduct might be if sufficiently egregious. And she was an attorney who understood the subtle definitions of crime; wasn't there an obligation of some sort on her part to report a major crime?

But murder? What is a word of this character doing in my medical clinic, or in any medical article not focused on forensic medicine? "How significant was this? What could the word "murder" mean here?" I kept asking myself.

There was slang use, of course, but that didn't seem to apply in any way I could push it. It could have just been invented – meaning a hyperbolic throw-away chosen for its color. Obviously, the likelihood of its having been of the bloody ax variety seemed slim, but versions of legal denial of treatment, or limiting critical access of some type, or denial of monies for treatment—bureaucratic killings, they might be called—were all valid possibilities in my mind.

But whatever it was, this lady-that-is-a-lawyer seemed to believe her insider knowledge about a major crime having been committed, and she was clear about wanting to make that point, whether or not I personally wanted knowledge of such a thing.

But what she did do that was consequential, was to give me a new sense of credibility with respect to the multiple dark stories of DOPL from the community that together seem to sense some massive and malevolent black hole directing traffic at the center of the DOPL galaxy.

Could this perilous comment of hers be made innocent if I pushed? I continued to ponder the possibilities she brought with her, but I came to realize that the only real pathway out of this was to label it a lie, or at least that she might have been wrong.

So was she lying? I doubt it. Or was she simply wrong? Maybe, but she's the attorney and the witness here. And besides, the murder—whatever this "murder"-that-was-also-a-Hollywood-MacGuffin was—it was also an insider DOPL thing that had nothing to do with or from me other than to provide the alert from this attorney that DOPL plays especially hard hardball...that it wishes to exert very forceful sway.

We had come to an agreement of sorts, so I stopped asking questions as they seemed to get intrusive, even though she had started a story that needed completion.

But she had lit up the night, my night anyway, and my mind wouldn't slow as I kept wondering about this woman.

Appropriately, I think, I found this Raymond Chandler injection of material into my simple medical life disconcerting. But please know that disconcerting is a very creepy word here.

Could her naming the crime and its perpetrator just be a straightforward way for her to tell me no? Or was this assertion in our office somehow satisfying her confusion about a proper course of action after having watched one's boss commit a murder but still wanting to continue working for him? And by telling the three of us about this supposed murder, are we now implicated if we don't rush into the DOPL front room screaming murder?

On the last point, please consider this letter a formal reporting on this abundantly strange situation.

After convincing me of her non-availability she went on to discuss other aspects of my situation, most specifically the supervisor killing grounds. Apparently, per this insider attorney, not being able to find a supervisor is—and has been for a number of years—a recognized hazard of interacting with DOPL and, further, is often utilized by DOPL as a ready tool for snipping off the ends of the careers of doctor's they simply don't like or find irascible, but who do not lend themselves to normal discipline. This last category seemed to be mine.

She had said it clearly and she had said it simply: the end of my medical license and medical career had been a planned event for the "supervisor-leave'em-hangin'" tool.

She added to that hugely morbid confession (we may call it) by noting her insider description that I recognized as thoroughly convincing by way of my personal insight that has come from my signing the confession; I—and the DOPL dark forces—alone know that there are no stipulations for which I was convicted, but there are contrived pastings of patient testimony that simulates negative legality as it stimulates dark force glee. So, when she describes this dark force as "chuckling as he cut and pasted patient accusations into the place for convictions," he and I alone understand the unique joy motivating his chuckle of cruelty that we might label his "chucklesomeness.

That image, of course, carries no legal weight, but the chuckling underlines the sadism as it validates the inclusion of the Scientific American article on psychopathy. But the murder, its openness, and the cultivated fear among the observers in this vague context are the real validators of likely psychopathy, just as the emptiness of Tim Hibler's accusation combine with the dark lawyer's accusation of the "supervisor-leave'em-hangin'" tool to reveal that my medical license destiny had from the beginning been planned to end in a dark closet filled with twisted ancient DOPL skeletons.

The purest of calculated fraud this, perpetrated upon what could easily be argued to be the most effective healing physician in Utah.

70% of patients treated with KISSD get 100 days of freedom from depression.

Psychiatry has simply never done it better, bless their fraudulent hearts.

No other physician in Utah, and probably the country, has better statistics for the treatment of depression, most specifically the psychiatrist Dr. Kendrick at the University of Utah who boasts truly terrible stats (Dr. Kendrick's clinic's longest depression interval of 28 days barely registers when compared to my clinic's longest at 14 months of depression freedom, for instance).

That's my respectable truth, DOPL's affliction, and Utah's dilemma. It is also an example of science revealing truth and healing through numbers.

And, of course, this is also much the country's dilemma, this populist denial of scientific truth. Donald and this dark force of DOPL would seem to have much in common.

Conclusion:

I came to Utah with an unsullied medical record after having practiced uneventfully for over twenty-five years in the most litigious state in the country, California.

I entered the ketamine world and found an unparalleled tool for treating depression, arguably the single worst disease known to Humankind. But ketamine was raw and remained undeveloped by either Big Pharma or psychiatry, as it should have been, and I found myself uniquely forced into a situation where I had to figure out this key antidepressant.

I did so, and I did so very effectively I say proudly, and was surprised in the process to find that ketamine was a far safer medicine at mental health doses than I, psychiatry, or anesthesiology had imagined.

This safety at low doses is a ketamine truth almost as valuable to the general treatment of depression, anxiety and PTSD as the KISSD process itself.

Again, let me boast proudly that, over the past 7 years, 4500 patients have received over 98,000 treatments without a major medical event. And remember that 70% of those have experienced what is likely the most effective reduction in depression that Humankind has ever known.

And know that to question this last statement, one must bring along an adequately peer-reviewed study.

Developing the KISSD protocol to provide literally the apex treatment for depression was an honor and a joy that few physicians on the planet—for very good reason—are ever pressed to experience. But with much luck, I confess, I succeeded, and the "70% of patients treated with KISSD get 100 days of freedom from depression" represents an unrivalled efficacy that is massively and determinedly rejected by psychiatry, to their deep, eternal, and venal disgrace.

For two years, then, DOPL searched for error but found none. They decided to take me to court anyway. No merit, no tort, but plenty of faulty allegiance to the local institution guaranteed their way.

Then Covid altered things to carnival level depravity where Judge Dibb promised to bark and spit mucous and Covid aerosol onto one and all. But I signed the note to keep infection rates down.

Then came the "supervisor-leave'em-hangin' tool", the DOPL legal maiden mumbling murder, and I'm still slowly twisting in this Utah desert wind.

Here we are or, at least, I am. Where is this to go?

Consequences

In medicine far more than in politics (but there, too) when we choose paths that do not follow the facts or figures of the matter, we soon get into trouble. Here, in the depression world, the difference of efficacy between the SSRIs of psychiatry and mental health ketamine is enormous.

Trying, as DOPL is doing here, to follow the proven-to-be-inferior SSRIs over ketamine at the direction of psychiatry is far more negative than a fool's errand; it is a scientific – and therefore moral - wrong. Anne Harrington laid this out clearly in her multiple New England Journal of Medicine (NEJM) articles on depression and SSRI's, as well as her book, *The Mind Fixers,* which is also quoted often in the NEJM.

Psychiatry has spent the last two decades pushing SSRIs with which they have maintained a sort of adulterer's relationship, in that it was only marginally effective and ridden with dangerous side effects, but there was nothing else that lent itself to psychiatry's "pill- a-day" convenience schema, most notably ketamine with its needs for parenteral administration. But where ketamine works for the patient, SSRIs work mostly for the doctor in a money sense and in a pill-a-day convenience sense.

Ketamine requires patient hand-holding by the physician. That hand-holding is what discourages psychiatry from utilizing this most appropriate of antidepressant medicines. A "negative type of freedom" in the Timothy Snyder sense allows psychiatry to utilize inferior SSRIs over ketamine. But the scientific facts give us figures that reveal the use of SSRIs by psychiatry to be part of a great institutional, money- oriented lie.

Lies of this sort are far more common in politics, which is where Timothy Snyder is focused for these comments on fact and truth-finding from his inspirational book, *On Freedom,* from which this quote is taken:

Freedom is the value of values, because it is what allows that difference to reside in us and in the world we make around us. Each of us has the right to a freedom that allows us to learn, choose, and combine values. We are not the same, but in the most essential sense, we are equal.

ON Freedom, Timothy Snyder, Crown New York 2024

And now, my justice…?

I would assert that my restriction from patients, my personal condemnation to poverty level for 4 years, the multiple hits on my reputation, and knowledge that DOPL is forcing depression, anxiety, PTSD and suicide onto the populace in ever greater numbers has been… what, adequate, sufficient enough(?) punishment?

And don't forget…there was no definable wrong committed by me.

And again, please don't forget that all the depression numbers are getting worse. That's why the state of Utah made psilocybin and MDMA legal a year ago. That they are not producing these healing agents that are somewhat controversial after their having promised them— while numbers continue to worsen—speaks to either confusion or MAGA redirection or simple bad intention (perhaps even money issues???).

So, I've suffered enough, ministers of DOPL. Please return my license, and then we can return to healing patients again. The depression numbers are surging, and I must repeat again and again that my process KISSD has the best depression treatment numbers in the history of Humankind.

This advice is to be ignored only at significant cost to the patient population out there.

We all know what should be done; please do it. Let me back in and I will have most of them smiling again in six months. No one else in the state of Utah can make that promise.

I assure you that I can both promise to heal them, and then do the job effectively.

To Summarize:

DOPL in the beginning days with Inspector Hibler was no more than an interested observer being directed by the avaricious-as-jealous Dr. Kendrick (and possibly his university associate, Dr. Salzburger) at the University of Utah.

Once the trial had been subverted, DOPL instituted the truly fraudulent and evil "supervisor-leave'em-hangin'" tool to nullify, obliterate, and make infamous my cherished and hugely moral medical license.

To see evil from this point of view is as revelatory as disgusting.

PART III

The Practice of Ketamine

Part III comprises the chapters originally intended for this practical book on providing an environment for treating depression with the unique and mighty medicine ketamine that comes with its own varied and unique list of needs. Most of this part is self-explanatory by way of the table of contents, but a few specific mentions are in order. Part II deals with the practical medical subtleties of running a ketamine clinic utilizing KISSD, the only medical tool to consistently abate the fearsome and foul LHBM (Lateral Habenular Burst Mode) , our single greatest foe to happiness and general well-being.

Chapter 16 is key to establishing the validity of the KISSD process as a uniquely effective delivery system for ketamine. As scientists, we are statisticians; this chapter continues an ongoing discussion about the best way to deliver ketamine. It will not be the last word, but it serves as a beginning in establishing consistent access to the 3-month interval of relative freedom from depression that I term the "Holy Grail of Depression". To my knowledge, no other pharmacologic entity or process—including other delivery modes for ketamine—can offer this extended period of normalcy that is the Holy Grail of Depression. Only transcranial magnetic therapy (TSM) suggests success at comparable rates.

Chapters 21 and 22, addressing Ketamine SLC's clinical treatment protocols and the consent form provided to all patients, covers much material discussed elsewhere. The reason for this is that these are meant to be available for use by other clinics as presented; they are there for themselves rather than the information they provide. As such entities are included exactly as utilized in the clinic on a day- to-day basis.

CHAPTER 11

Ketamine Data and the Significance of R3

In Dr. Steven J. Hyde's technically excellent book, "Ketamine for Depression," chapter 3 has nearly 40 pages devoted to a review of every significant article on utilizing ketamine for depression published between 2000 and 2018. All of the articles are somewhat timid in that the numbers of patients are never large. Dr. Hyde also mentions that, especially the earlier articles, even though they showed remarkably positive results and much therapy with few side effects, their impact on modern medicine was always minimal, especially in the halls of Big Pharma. Where this comes from is a voluminous subject not appropriate for this note, other than to accept that there is an operative agenda related to money at high levels.

Over the 18 years the investigators consistently assert the following:

1. That ketamine is remarkably effective.
2. That ketamine treatments at these sub-anesthetic levels enjoy an exceptionally low level of significant side effects.
3. That multiple doses of the "standard protocol ketamine dose" of 0.5 mg/kg IV over 40 minutes lengthen the intervals of freedom-from-depression.

Very importantly, what they do not assert or determine is that the total dosage of the combined treatments is the single most significant parameter in defining interval length. This is where our intramuscular system, KISSD, gains huge ground relative to the understandably tentative intravenous mode of administration. KISSD allows the same milligramage of ketamine to be administered in a single day that, intravenously, could not be administered even with the six treatments administered on different days.

It is this single parameter which allows me to assert that my clinic utilizing the system of KISSD is the cheapest, safest, and most effective method of administering ketamine in America. Now, when I say this, I am mostly thinking of infusion clinics which currently define the vast majority of ketamine clinics.

Useful Ketamine Treatment Parameters

1. "Feels good/depression decreases" during treatment.
   a. Generally "enjoys the high."
   b. The "high" is not the goal.
   c. Though not the goal, enjoying the high suggests an increased likelihood of future antidepression benefits.

2. Response Rate
   a. Response rate typically defined as a 50% decrease in symptoms at 24 hours.
   b. "Interval length" implicitly uses response rate in its definition in that the definition of interval length is response rate over time.

3. PHQ-9 changes large and small, and both immediate and over time. Are there implications in treatment or response for the following varieties of change?
   a. Start high, ending low, meaning back to a normal value.
   b. Start with middle values and improve to normal values.
   c. Start high, but progress to only middle values; how much depression and danger remain? What else can we look at to complement this parameter?

4. Interval Length.
   a. 3 to 6 months = "Holy Grail of Depression."
   b. 1 to 3 months = good, sometimes acceptable as an endpoint, but needs to be tested to ensure that no improvement available with increasing dose.
   c. One month is a common interval that is an especially prominent dividing line; higher dosing can very often improve this value.
   d. Significantly less than one month.
      1. Ketamine troches will almost certainly be the mainstay of treatment with periodic parenteral injections as needed to address episodes of worsening depression.
      2. Do PHQ-9's, combined with the "style" of ketamine troche consumption, give us any insights into future success or failure, especially suicide?

Ketamine Troches

1. PHQ-9's ability to predict; are there any differences in their use with troches versus parenteral administration?
2. Is there any pattern of PHQ-9 change and additional parenteral ketamine usage that might predict untoward changes?
3. The hoped-for response of ketamine troches is that over time the intervals will gradually increase until, ideally, the patient enjoys remission = equals normalcy.

CHAPTER 12

The Four Modes of Ketamine Efficacy

The Four Modes of Ketamine Efficacy in The Treatment of Depression, Anxiety and PTSD

Whereas the modes of action of SSRIs and SNRIs are either unknown or simply nonexistent, ketamine has a formidable list of scientifically validated facts which contribute to the spectacular depression relief that we see with ketamine. Those four modes are:

1. The psychedelia manifesting dissociation.
2. Relief from lateral habenular burst mode.
3. Multiple mechanisms of dendritic repair.
4. An ill-defined relationship with the body's internal opiate system as revealed in a recent naltrexone study at Stanford.

We will discuss these four mechanisms separately.

Psychedelia

From the Nixon years, way back when Timothy Leary's LSD, magic mushrooms, and Don Juan's psychedelic cacti were all legal, medical studies showed that these entities had positive effects on depression; they worked. But their effects were limited; relief was not total, it was very limited in duration, and the drugs themselves do not lend themselves to easy administration in our complex, modern world. These drugs are seeing a resurgence in interest, but I've seen nothing to suggest that they duplicate the multiple mechanisms that make ketamine such a profoundly unique and valuable drug. They will almost certainly find some valuable role in the medical treatment of depression, but that role will be limited and will be unlikely to be casually available in the near future.

So, does the psychedelia of ketamine play a significant role in its depression relief? We don't really know, mostly because ketamine's other effects are profound and powerful, making conceptual separation of their effects difficult. My guess is that the psychedelia does make a contribution and many ketamine practitioners believe they see increasingly positive results with increasing psychedelic effect. Future examiners will, I'm sure, define this question further. But I can say that many treatment sessions have demonstrated increasing treatment effect of both depression and anxiety with increasing dose. Is it the psychedelia or some other parameter of the circulating chemical that is causing the effect?

An answer to this question could possibly come from a comparison study to the current propofol investigation going on at the University. Where investigators currently administer 10 propofol anesthesias to effect their treatment, I would suggest that a single ketamine anesthesia (termed a "ketamine coma" in this context) could produce the same benefits. This study would also lend itself to answering the academic question about the role of psychedelia in treating depression.

Lateral Habenular Burst-Mode Abatement

In what I would assert to be the core defining article in all of depression literature, the February 15, 2018 issue of Nature Magazine has three articles on the topic of ketamine and depression. In the central article they first assert that ketamine is the most significant contribution to all of psychiatry in the past 50 years. They then define the lateral habenula as being our brain organ of despair and depression, actions that it accomplishes primarily by suppression of reward centers.

Suddenly, in this article, depression becomes very much a disease of anatomy.

The lateral habenula sits immediately in front of the pineal gland and is about the same size. The lateral habenula apparently measures every bit of stress experienced by its brain system, and when that brain system reaches its uniquely defined tipping point, a small focus of lateral habenular neurons takes that information and fires off the lateral habenular burst mode in theta-band synchronization. This burst mode then courses through the brain, signaling it to enter the naturally selected personal catastrophe that is depression.

The article has actual photographs of this burst mode in the lateral habenula before it communicates a message of depression to the rest of the brain. After forty years of hearing references to "the chemical imbalance of depression" without ever having seen a measured imbalance, it is extremely refreshing to see those clusters of 5 to 6 neuronal beats standing out as clearly as a billboard on the freeway, and know that you are actually looking at depression.

And what, specifically, is messaged to the brain? Undoubtedly, a new brain state of fight or flight is called up and, coincident to that, we see the three reward centers shut down:

1. The ventral tegmental area shuts down so that we get little dopamine.
2. The dorsal raphe nucleus becomes hypoactive such that we get less serotonin.
3. And the rostral medial tegmental nucleus squeezes down to compromise our GABA (gamma aminobutyric acid).

This series of events is what constitutes the bulk of the experience of depression, though depression can have many other varieties of expression in any given individual.

And ketamine reverses these effects in minutes. We see this in the mice with their habenular cameras showing burst mode abatement, and we see it in the pattern of response in our patients who often experience dramatic transitions from their depression as we watch them change before us.

"This is where we get our born-again-Christian level of joy," I like to say to patients as I'm showing them the article's photographs of burst mode abatement, "Have your hallelujah ready," for this moment is very often one of glowing spirituality embedded in a joy that no depressed patient has seen in a long time.

To know this release from depression that is granted by ketamine is a special experience; there are few, if any, events on the planet that are its equivalent. This is another way of saying that the only way to know and understand the true depths of depression is to have experienced them first-hand.

Dendritic Repair

We have known for many years that ketamine stimulates the mTOR (mammalian target of rapamycin) pathway to promote neurogenesis and the repair of dendrites in the hippocampus. This suggests a possible explanation for the consistently poor memory in depressed personalities.

Recently, an article was presented by way of National Public Radio that discussed the results of a study where a two-stage dendritic repair process was observed in neurons in areas of the brain reflecting stress. Those areas were not defined, but the description of the dendritic alterations suggested neuronal repair that was initially partial in nature, followed later by full replacement of the dendrite.

The concept of dendritic repair, where every neuron in a human brain connects to a thousand other neurons by way of dendrites, becomes one of maintenance and would, therefore, be one to be hoped for. Dendrites in this capacity essentially take on the role of mortar in a brick wall; it's everywhere - of course, we want it done right. This would seem to be the rough equivalent of changing the oil in your car.

Ketamine's discovery as a stimulator of dendritic repair in a world where we recognize no others, then, would seem to have no negative consequences. Yay to dendritic repair.

Access to the Body's Internal Opiate System

Within the last year, a study at Stanford involving ketamine's effects in the presence of naltrexone, suggested that ketamine's antidepressant effects were abated by the naltrexone. So completely, in fact, that the study had to be discontinued.

There were hints in the media that this suggested some kind of untoward behavior on the part of ketamine that suggested a relationship with opiates that might prove negative. I have heard nothing more of the article and the comments about an opiate relationship have faded away, though some kind of unique relationship with opiates seems likely. After all, ketamine can play an immensely positive role in the area of opiate addiction, suggesting that any revealed mechanism of ketamine's relationship to opiates would be explanatory rather than accusatory.

Ketamine has a major role to play in our opiate crisis. An opiate addict's withdrawal symptoms can be completely abated with ketamine.

But, ketamine also reduces an opiate addict's tolerance to zero, presenting a major treatment dilemma in high dose opiate addiction. We have not figured out how to introduce ketamine into the world of opiate addiction, almost certainly for the same reasons that ketamine has been suppressed in the world of depression treatment for the past 15 years - namely the billions of dollars that come from SSRIs.

Those billions keep SSRIs flowing as, in equal proportion, those same billions maintain a steady flow of ketamine criticism.

Adding up the stress diseases of depression, anxiety and PTSD, there are between 60 and 120 million (adding the kids in) sufferers of stress diseases that could benefit from ketamine. If this is true, it is not too difficult to describe America's current feedlot relationship with anti-depression medications as the greatest moral failing in the history of mankind.

Next, we will discuss KISSD – Ketamine Intramuscular Stepped

System for Depression - a system of ketamine administration that lends itself to both flexible dosing and an atmosphere ready and willing to address the full range of emergence reactions that will naturally attend any clinic that offers genuinely adequate ketamine dosing.

CHAPTER 13

KISSD: Ketamine Intramuscular Stepped System for Depression

The historical administration of ketamine has been tied to its, until recently, nearly exclusive role in the operating room as a general anesthetic. As such, that operating room role has defined both how ketamine is given and how it is to be viewed in terms of side effects, adverse events during treatment, and constraints on its administration. This "OR mentality" has resulted in a maintenance of the primary mode of administration, namely intravenous as opposed to intramuscular or other routes, which has led to serious constraints on dosage, safety of administration, and price. In an epidemic situation where insurance does not cover the product, price can deny millions of suffering Americans access to relief from what is arguably the worst disease known to man, depression and its close relatives, anxiety and PTSD.

There is a progression of safety in the administration of ketamine when moving through the primary modes of administration. Safety, when administering ketamine, is concerned with the likelihood of occurrence of one of five primary adverse events: apnea, hypertension, hypotension, glottic spasm and emergence reactions. The first four entities are all major medical concerns because of the mortality and morbidity which they can inflict; they can all kill you.

The likelihood of these four adverse events diminishes when we move from intravenous administration to intramuscular administration, and probably from intramuscular administration to ketamine troches, which are lozenges that dissolve in the cheek and are almost certainly the future of ketamine. This question of intravenous versus intramuscular ketamine is an important one and will be discussed in greater depth later.

The fifth concern, emergence reactions of ketamine, are an entirely different phenomenon from its other adverse events which are genuinely medical events; the emergence reaction is more a behavioral or psychologic phenomenon than it is a medical threat. Emergence reactions are essentially the stories of bad trips, freak outs and similar psychedelia-related experiences that have always plagued ketamine as a problem related to anesthesia. But with its utilization as an antidepressant, the nature of the treatment dictates that the patient is conscious during most of the procedure which means that the psychedelia is much more prominent. Consequently, it suffers much from simple cultural comparisons to the likes of magic mushrooms and LSD which have been disparaged since the times of Nixon. But, aside from the cultural problems, emergence reactions do pose very genuine difficulties.

The specter of emergence reactions, defined generally as psychedelicized patients suddenly running amok and confused in a heavily instrumented operating room environment, is an obviously frightening one that hugely influences ketamine dosage and its consequent perceptions of safety. Emergence reactions constitute the primary argument against intravenous ketamine and is a controversial and hugely misunderstood subject which will be given its own chapter later in this writing. I will jump ahead to say, however, that the intramuscular route hugely diminishes negative concerns for emergence reactions with a protocol approach that very much contains the problem.

The stepped system of intramuscular ketamine that we have named KISSD allows for an aggressive, and therefore therapeutic, dose of ketamine to be administered in a careful, sensitive, repeatable and understandable-to-the-patient manner that gives the patient a sense of measure and place in a psychedelic experience that is normally fraught with confusion and disorientation.

I term this "creating an ally," which is a concept stolen from Carlos Casteneda, an author of a series of books telling stories of a shaman teaching a neophyte nerd his native American magic through drugs. Learning of the drugs is termed "creating an ally;" the KSSD system does create allies as patients move through its processes. And as I depart from that strange world of shamanism and the negative baggage of drugs in the 60s, thoughts of "tripping for the sake of tripping," in this modern ketamine context should be discarded; they simply are not the same experience and ketamine as a medical entity is one of the most valuable mental health tools ever presented to psychiatry.

What is a step?

A step in this ketamine treatment scenario is a repeating unit of treatment that allows a patient to get a sense of measure and proportion from her ketamine treatment which, as a psychedelic experience, is extremely difficult to define, measure, understand or make decisions from. To understand this in any way other than to have the ketamine

experience itself, we must go back to the beginning when we first came to the knowledge that ketamine was indeed the exalted treatment for depression, anxiety and PTSD that it is.

In the beginning, at that moment 20 years ago when we realized that this general anesthetic called ketamine was a great antidepressant, we knew three things about ketamine that defined most of how it was to be given for the next 15 years.

The three most important things that we knew about ketamine were:

1. Ketamine had a remarkably relieving effect on depression.
2. Ketamine was a psychedelic.
3. Ketamine, as a psychedelic, could lead to very troubling freak outs or bad trips; these have been termed emergence reactions since the early days of ketamine anesthesia.

These freak outs understandably freaked out the physicians charged with managing them. Recognizing that total dose and rate of administration were key elements in determining the likelihood of emergence reactions, the initial dose of recommended ketamine for depression was determined to be approximately 1/120th of a standard anesthetic dose.

That now hallowed dose that most ketamine centers begin with, and that many others will not go beyond, is:

Protocol initial ketamine dose = 0.5 mg per kilogram given IV over 40 minutes.

At this dose, very few people have emergence reactions, though it is not unheard of. At this dose, most patients will note a level of reaction that they would characterize as moderate and pleasant, with very few experiencing psychedelic colors or distortions of reality. In my experience with over 2,000 patients where I've started with that dose, I've noted a total of only four reactions that I would characterize as negative in a major, "bad trip" or "freak out" sense (nausea, moderate confusion we would call negative also, but they would be put into what we would call a minor or lesser category, none of these being formal terms) . Of those four, only one episode was sufficiently uncomfortable to prompt the patient to discontinue ketamine treatment on the basis of that single first dose.

If we restrict ourselves to that miniscule 1/120th of an anesthetic dose, which is 0.5 mg/kg, but give multiple sequential, non-overlapping doses of ketamine, we get the following treatment responses from a "normal" depressed brain (meaning that the patient does not suffer their depression from one of the following entities: bipolarity, OCD, pain-based depression, autism.

Non-overlapping doses of 0.5 mg/kg over 40 min.	Expected Duration of Freedom from Depression
1	10-12 days
2	3 weeks
4	6 weeks
6	12 weeks

Expected Duration of Effect from Multiples of the Protocol Ketamine Dose.

From this table we glean a great truth relating to this very unique treatment profile. Despite the fact that ketamine has a very short duration of immediate medicine effect, this pharmacologic agent in the receptive brain can effectively dissolve depression like it was an angry spot on your white T-shirt in a "Tide" commercial. That treated depression will then remain at bay for three months or longer, bestowing upon ketamine a supremely unique pharmacologic status in the world of depression.

This fact, along with ketamine's undeniable safety record, is why nature magazine designated ketamine as the most significant contribution to psychiatry in the past 50 years.

But the table must be qualified because it applies *only to the approximately 40% of depressed personalities who find that their minds respond ideally to parenteral ketamine* and who consequently go on to enjoy freedom from depression for intervals as long as 2-3 months. Another approximately 40% of these patients will see their depression respond, but their freedom from depression intervals will range from days to a week or two. These are candidates more likely to find benefit with ketamine troches or other oral preparations taken daily or weekly. To these we must add the non-responders that usually include from 10 to 30% of those depressed minds treated with ketamine.

There are very happy consequences to this unique activity which are not always currently utilized with extant treatment regimens. As I will be discussing, KFD SLC's stepped system of ketamine administration maximizes ketamine's benefits when reaching for durations of effect which can stretch to as long as 12 weeks (though I have a number of patients who maintain depression-free states for seven to eight months with no depression).

Most ketamine practices begin with the dosage calculation given above: 0.5 mg/kg IV over 40 minutes. This dose and the efforts to define it was initiated at Yale 20 years ago. How did they arrive at the regimen of a dose every two days for six doses?

I would like to insert here that these individual doses are reminiscent of the "step" of our system of stepped ketamine, but they are not at all the same. More on this later.

Our job now is to decide how those first practitioners decided to give those 6 ketamine doses of 0.5 mg per kilogram. We have four possible patterns of administration:

1. We could give them all at once for a dose of 3.0 mg/kg IV over 40 minutes.

   But this immediately defies our freak-out avoidance mandate; surely many patients would, indeed, freak out with an emergence reaction at this maximized regimen.
2. Ketamine's half-life of 20 minutes means that the peak of the experience occurs at 15 to 18 minutes with a trough at 30 minutes, at which time the next dose may be given. We could, then, give these six doses sequentially 30 minutes apart.

   This could theoretically work. And, in fact, our stepped system will eventually give sequential doses in just this fashion and for just as many doses, and they will have a much higher "milligramage" with each dose which will very often result in enhanced therapeutic effect.

   But this brand-new patient is not yet acclimated; she is not yet a psychonaut (another term to be forgiven by the therapeutically oriented,) and would be very likely to suffer an emergence reaction if given these six doses in a row.

So, we don't do this.

3. The next option for the six doses is to give one dose a day for the total of 6. This works very well, and for people that fly in from out of town that don't want to spend 12 days in Salt Lake City, it works extremely well.

   But, for patients that live locally, coming into the clinic for this treatment every day for six days in a row is, for most people, simply too congested. They just don't like it.
4. So, we add an empty day between the treatment days such that now the protocol ketamine course is six treatments in 12 days and the patient is happy, especially if he gets a three month interval ("interval" is a much focused-on term in our practice; "maximizing the interval" is our constant goal).

Here we have a regimen that works, and we see the beginnings of patient happiness through ketamine. And the doctor? Well, the doctor gets to charge the patient six times, bless his heart, of course he's happy.

Ketamine for Depression Salt Lake City is the cheapest ketamine in America (and I use that word "cheap" proudly, knowing that we utilize the same ketamine as every other physician in America, and do it with a procedure that confers both high safety and success) for two reasons:

1. Our $300 price is among the lowest in America all by itself.
2. Our system of condensing the standard six treatments into a single session means that we are effectively 1/6 that $300 price relative to other clinics who require those *six treatments with each treatment series.*

Our stepped system of ketamine administration allows us to build up the dosage in a slow, graduated, patient-involving manner that allows maximal rate of relief from depression as it also maximizes the following depression-free interval.

The concept of an induced depression-free interval from the depths of actual major depression is the "holy grail" of all of depression therapy. In the past, isoflurane general anesthesia, and now, propofol general anesthesia, offer much the same end result but require the massive technology, personnel, and funds of an operating room.

Depression-relief for a maximized interval as long as three months is a promise that currently only ketamine can safely, cheaply and consistently offer.

This "holy grail" is also an entity which seems to be pursued less and less in the modern ketamine clinic, despite its remaining as the ultimate goal for any person suffering from depression. From what I've seen recently (mostly from the recent national ketamine conference in Denver, hosted by ASKP), the initial six doses are often given, but to maintain the approach of a series of six ketamine treatments every three months can be both expensive in itself and difficult to fit into a busy schedule.

KFD SLC pursues the holy grail of ketamine depression therapy while remaining proudly the cheapest ketamine in America. Our process essentially condenses those six doses of ketamine into a single treatment session which, in turn, maximizes both the immediate treatment response as well as the resultant depression-free interval.

The intramuscular approach is key to both safe administration and close patient participation in the procedure. We will now define the process by which we safely create a psychonaut which is then capable of entertaining a ketamine dose appropriate to obtaining the holy Grail of depression therapy, the three-month, ketamine-induced, depression free interval.

We use the initial six treatment sessions, but only once, condensing the six sessions in the process to a single entity for which we charge the same $300. This we assert, is how you treat a national-level epidemic of depression and anxiety which we are now facing. This is how you treat 80 million depressed Americans; these numbers demand attention and a certain amount of aggressiveness which we are starting to see, I think, everywhere.

In general, there is much turmoil among institutions whose bottom line is tied to the continued flow of SSRIs, usually defined by their financial ties to big Pharma entities; this leaves few academic institutions in America able to participate adequately in this new mental health world defined by ketamine.

To those involved in the turmoil, might I please refer you to the October 31 New England Journal of Medicine where the current psychiatry - Big Pharma "identity crisis" has hugely muddied the depression-anxiety mental health world.

I literally gasped as the New England Journal asserted that, "Psychiatry should be uniquely positioned to help with this crisis through example, scholarship, and consultation, yet the field seems to have largely abandoned its social, interpersonal, and psychodynamic foundations, with little to show for the sacrifices."

Ann Harrington, a medical historian quoted in the article, proposed that, "psychiatry limit its scope to severe, mostly psychotic disorders." This, I would interpret, means that psychiatrists limit themselves to in-hospital practices where those extremes of psychoses are to be found. This reflects the many years of moneyed obsession with SSRIs directed ineffectively, or even harmfully, at patients diagnosed with mild and moderate depression *where SSRIs have not been shown to be effective.*

Despite psychiatrists' concern with the ebullience of the modern ketamine world - or, perhaps, *because* of psychiatrists' concern with our ebullience (remember, there is an epidemic out there with 80 million depressed people suffering the worst disease known to man) - getting this word out to those who may benefit is one of the most important imperatives of our times.

So, on that note, onward to the most effective entity in America for delivering ketamine to her depressed and oppressed millions.

KISSD - Ketamine Intramuscular Stepped System for Depression.

We begin, then, with the seminal protocol formula for treating depression with ketamine:

Protocol initial ketamine dose = 0.5 mg per kilogram given IV over 40 minutes.

A key fact arises from this formula; whatever dose might be calculated from this formula, the table of duration of effect accumulating from the particular number of protocol doses administered, tells us that six doses will be required to reach the Holy Grail duration of three months.

The significance of this is that it tells us that the single day dosage required to get the patient to a three-month interval is six times that protocol dose. So, a 176-pound patient calculates to 80 kg and a 40 mg protocol ketamine dose.

This means that our target goal for a single booster dose must be six times this value or 240 mg; to qualify for a depression free interval of three months, this patient must receive 240 mg within the single session.

Our stepped system is a procedure of 13 steps administered over six sessions where each session except the last includes two injections 30 minutes apart, and where each injection, termed a "leg" in our parlance, sees an increase in dose of 10 mg. The increases culminate on the fifth session where the final, maximum dose, is used to construct the final "booster," our term for the sixth day's series of three injections.

So, the above patient, calculated to have a 40 mg initial protocol ketamine dose, would have a stepped system series of treatments that would look something like this:

Session #	Ketamine doses in milligrams	Total day's dose
1	35 mg, 45 mg	80 mg
2	55 mg, 65 mg	120 mg
3	75 mg, 85 mg	160 mg
4	95 mg, 105 mg	200 mg
5	110 mg, 120 mg	230 mg
6	120 mg, 120 mg, 120 mg	360 mg

Two things to note here.

First, on day one we started with the dosage slightly less than the protocol amount. This we do simply to be gentle.

Second, note that only session six's booster dose of three 120 mg injections surpasses the 240 mg mark noted earlier as the dose necessary to qualify for the holy Grail three-month interval.

During this series, each individual step is an opportunity for patient interrogation, input, and treatment alteration. A patient is never moved to the next level without first questioning her and obtaing acquiescence to the regimen. More on this in a later chapter.

Let us continue now with our progress in the institution of this ketamine regimen.

The patient has at this stage received a full series of ketamine and is now under the expectation that she will have a three-month period free of the depression that has undoubtedly plagued her for years. Unfortunately, that promise is not granted to the majority of ketamine recipients. The three-month interval does require a certain minimal amount of ketamine, usually approximating the six initial protocol ketamine treatments.

But even with that appropriate amount of ketamine, only about 40% of patients will get three months of freedom from depression; the rest, we assume, does not reach that interval secondary to having the "wrong kind of brain." From practical experience, we know that if you have one of these "wrong brains," you simply will not get that three-month interval. A "wrong brain" would be one that included a mental health diagnoses of bipolarity, obsessive-compulsive disease, chronic pain, autism, and undoubtedly a few others that have yet to be defined.

So, how do we deal with this disparity? First, after completion of the 3-injection booster, we let them go to conduct their lives with their new normalcy in hand, letting them know that we simply do not know ourselves how long their newly healthy brain will last.

If they last the hoped-for three full months, our calculations are finished. The proposed regimen will be that three-legged booster dose of 360 mg every three months for $300, forever. Patient variations will, of course, occur and they will be dealt with intuitively at each juncture. Some will drop off in the measure of their success and drop out of the ketamine program; they will require other approaches.

But for most in this most exalted of post-depression situations, life is a series of wonders as life should be, and it comes with the first-hand knowledge of how dark life can be. Paul Thoreau, the travel author, once said that one of human beings' most ironic difficulties was the art of, at a moment of happiness, actually recognizing that you are so. I would suggest that a prior depressive that has been released from his depression by ketamine has an especially good chance of appreciating his own genuine happiness at the moment of its experience.

If 40% of the ketamine-treated reach three months, 60% do not. What do we do with them? These patients generally divide themselves into two groups; one of them lives with depression free intervals lasting from one to two months and continues with variations of the ketamine booster we saw above. The other will advance to ketamine troches (dissolvable cheek lozenges capable of delivering high doses - the future of ketamine).

The mechanics of how this works are as follows. If the patient should return at four weeks, my first response would be to add one more leg, meaning that if he had received the three 120 mg injections as his initial booster, then I would add a leg. By this I mean that he would get four 120 mg injections and we would see if it gave him another week of interval, such that he had a five-week interval. If that happened, I would give him another leg still, for five 120 mg doses and see if we didn't get six weeks.

It's all about the interval.

And if the patient only lasted one to two weeks? I would give the patient the four-legged booster as above but, knowing that this was going to be a poor patient to pursue with ketamine injections, I would start him on ketamine troches and assume that that would be his future.

Ketamine troches can deliver effectively the same dosages that we give parenterally, and they are given at home, usually with a chaperone. They can be broken up and taken in any range of dosing. In higher doses there is a definite fall risk from the instability. It approximates that of opiates but, of course, is far safer than opiates owing to its virtual freedom-from-apnea risk. Troches and their practical administration will be discussed in a later chapter.

Ketamine is available intravenously, intramuscularly, as ketamine troches, and as a nasal spray. We've discussed the 13-step system of ketamine administration and we've mentioned ketamine troches. But most of medical ketamine continues to be administered as it has been for decades in the operating room - through an IV. Doctors tend to be creatures of tradition and tradition certainly seems to be ruling here.

But is it appropriate?

Most of the time, I would think not, but this viewpoint is not yet commonly held. Let us now discuss that traditional world of intravenous ketamine versus its less constrained challenger from the world of intramuscular ketamine

CHAPTER 14

Intravenous vs Intramuscular Ketamine

As the field of treating distressed diseases of depression, anxiety and PTSD is evolving toward ketamine, the preferences for various potential routes of administration of ketamine are also evolving. Ketamine is a drug developed as a general anesthetic where its primary use has been in providing general anesthesia from inside the operating room. As such, the operating room has always dictated that an intravenous line be in place. The reasons for an IV in the operating room are multiple, going beyond simple administration of medicines to include fluid administration and a few other procedures.

The recognition that ketamine is incredibly and uniquely effective at treating depression, anxiety and PTSD has brought ketamine out of the operating room to address these issues. Currently, ketamine is administered most often through an intravenous line (IV), though it is also administered by intramuscular (IM) injection, ketamine lozenges and by ketamine nasal spray.

The world of depression is currently fraught with competing interests involving appropriate treatment of the disease on one side and, on the other, money. This conflict comes from the huge cash flows associated with minimally effective SSRIs being threatened by generic, dirt-cheap ketamine. This is an important story of conflict between Big Pharma and ketamine practitioners everywhere, and I discuss it in greater detail elsewhere in this writing.

This route of administration issue that we are currently discussing, though, arises mostly inside the world of ketamine for depression. As mentioned above, most ketamine for depression is administered by intravenous line. This is a product of both habit and tradition. Doctors are by nature conservative and traditional; if an IV has been used in the past for a given procedure, then it is likely that an IV will be used for the same procedure for the same benefits in the future.

But, if other routes have unique benefits, they should be considered. I assert that there is a progression in general safety when moving from intravenous to intramuscular to ketamine troche and on to ketamine nasal spray. This note will make that case, primarily in discussing intravenous versus intramuscular ketamine where the issues of concern focus on the anesthetic history of ketamine that asserts that because the procedure was done that way in the past, it should therefore be done that way in the future.

Intravenous Ketamine < Intramuscular < Ketamine Troche
→ Increasing Safety →

In fact, as we shall see, the actual ketamine insert itself - the description of the drug's properties that accompany it in the actual delivery box - points out that the intravenous delivery of ketamine is associated with a higher frequency of adverse events such that, in a non-OR situation such as the circumstances we see in clinics treating depression, anxiety and PTSD with ketamine, *the intravenous route is associated with a higher rate of adverse events than the intramuscular.*

My personal experience confirms that observation.

That having been said, I will go farther still and assert that for the majority of users the future of ketamine will utilize the ketamine troche, a safer and far more convenient mode of delivery than either the intravenous or intramuscular routes; with ketamine troches we can give ketamine safely at home in significant doses.

Intravenous vs Intramuscular Ketamine

I will be discussing this issue from three general points of view:

1. Adverse Events - the pharmaceutical approach where we compare the likelihoods of inducing major adverse events while giving ketamine in intravenous vs intramuscular modes.
2. The Emergence Reaction - unique role of the emergence reaction in compromising the use of intravenous ketamine in treating depression, anxiety or PTSD.
3. Cost - the role of money as a filter in denying ketamine to those most in need.

Adverse Events:

What is known as the "Insert" is a small body of data supplied by the pharmaceutical company manufacturing the product that contains information that the company deems critical to proper medical utilization of the drug. In many ways it comprises the most fundamentally valid information about the product that is available; it represents a summation by the people who did the original pharmaceutical work on the drug.

The insert accompanying the packaged ketamine is entitled, "Ketamine Hydrochloride Injection, USP." Within that insert are the following quotes arranged by chief element of pathologic concern which includes emergence reactions, glottic spasm, respiratory depression, and hypertension.

Emergence Reactions:

1. "Emergence reactions have occurred in approximately 12% of patients."
2. "They are *less frequent when the drug is given intramuscularly*, and the incidence is reduced as experience with the drug is gained."
3. "The incidence of psychologic manifestations during emergence, particularly dream-like observations and emergence delirium, may be reduced by using lower recommended dosages of ketamine hydrochloride injection in conjunction with intravenous diazepam during induction and maintenance of anesthesia."
4. As discussed later, an emergence reaction is not in and of itself a life-threatening experience as the other three adverse events can be. But, with an IV in place, an emergence reaction presents an extremely unsettling experience to the physician; there will be blood.

Glottic Spasm:

"Laryngospasm and other forms of airway obstruction have occurred during ketamine hydrochloride injection anesthesia." This is a life-threatening event.

Respiratory Depression and Apnea:

1. Respiratory depression may occur with over dosage or too rapid a rate of administration of ketamine hydrochloride injection." This is, of course, a life-threatening event.
2. "The intravenous dose should be administered over a period of 60 seconds. More rapid administration may result in respiratory depression or apnea and enhanced pressure response."
3. "Although respiration is frequently stimulated, severe depression of respiration or apnea may occur following rapid intravenous administration of high doses of ketamine hydrochloride injection."

Ketamine-induced Hypertension:

1. "Elevation of blood pressure begins shortly after injection, reaches a maximum within a few minutes, and usually returns to pre-anesthetic values within 15 minutes after injection. In most cases, the systolic and diastolic blood pressure peaks 10 to 50% above preanesthetic levels, but the elevation can be higher or longer in individual cases." Hypertension can, of course, also be a life-threatening event.
2. "The intravenous dose should be administered over a period of 60 seconds. More rapid administration may result in respiratory depression or apnea and enhanced presser response."

Though a few other conditions such as hypotension, increases in intraocular pressure, and bladder problems may occur, they are not in the forefront of concern as are the four entities mentioned above. The theme presented by the writers of the insert makes clear that three factors affect the likelihood of the appearance of the above-listed adverse events.

Those factors are:

1. Total dosage.
2. Rate of administration.
3. Intravenous administration produces more adverse events than intramuscular administration.

Increasing the dosage and increasing the rate of administration are concepts easily understood. Giving "more," or giving it faster intuitively produces more effect. But intravenous versus intramuscular is not so obvious. The ketamine insert does make the simple assertion that intramuscular ketamine results in fewer adverse events than intravenous, but it gives us no numbers to guide our sense of proportion.

A general point to note: An IV's primary source of danger is its easy potential for rapid delivery rate, whether that rate is intended or not; accidental overdoses can follow bad arithmetic very easily. But just giving the drug by the IV route, even at the appropriate rate, increases negative exposure because of the way the IV allows the drug to be dumped into the bloodstream where it barrels through the vasculature with shifting concentration gradients in a slurry that slams into the patient's heart, brain, or larynx in a fashion far more consequential than a typical intramuscular injection.

With an intramuscular injection, the drug first enters a muscle where it is slowed as it diffuses through the tissue before trickling into the bloodstream with little of the shock of the concentration gradients generated by the "open hose" of an intravenous line in a vein.

So, we have the insert asserting that, in a world where ketamine is given mostly through an IV, the intramuscular route is the safer of the two. But, now, we seem to have little academic data to define their differences.

All that I have to guide me is my own data.

In my personal practice of just over 2,000 patients and an estimated 8,400 treatment sessions over the past three years, I've had only one of the above-mentioned major adverse ketamine reactions occur; that event took place in a 15-year-old female that suffered an easy-to-control apnea with an O2 sat in the mid-40s. That event of apnea took place *during an intravenous treatment.*

Since that IV-related event of apnea, I've completed over 7,800 intramuscular sessions and *I've not suffered a single non-emergent, major adverse event.* This suggests an adverse event ratio of at least 10 to 1. If this 10 to 1 ratio were valid, the intramuscular route should be considered much safer. But we need more data to solidify that assertion; with a single statistical event such as this, we simply cannot make strong statements or come to firm conclusions without more data.

The data is available, however; the practitioners at the University of

Utah's ketamine clinic have the data, as do ketamine clinics elsewhere. The University has so far been reluctant to share their data. Perhaps, if the needs of the populace are properly expressed, they will. "Science is a communal effort, and we should default to being open and sharing," says Stanford's John P.A. Ioannidis, one of the country's strongest advocates for data integrity.

Emergence Reactions Compromise Effective Dosage with Intravenous Administration

Though untoward events include such dangerous entities as glottic spasm, apnea, and high blood pressure, the greatest practical demon of a practitioner of IV ketamine is arguably a behaviorally run-amuck patient.

Several months ago, I had, as a ketamine patient, an NFL defense end that was more cut than Lebron James. He was given a significant dose of intramuscular ketamine and, shortly after being given the medicine, began taking what looked like on-field, scrimmage-session practice rolls while looking confused and a little frightened. He repeated several times, "What's going on?" This continued for two or three minutes, during which time we guided him into Love Sacs and away from walls. In this classic emergence phenomenon event, the patient did well.

But, if he had had an IV in place, NO ONE could have stopped this athlete. Turning off the IV would be an option that the doctor would hope would be available, but what are the odds that the doctor would be quicker than an NFL defense end? A short-acting barbiturate would've been a happy answer, but ONLY if the IV was still present, a very doubtful outcome after the first shoulder role. Additionally, if the structure of our treatment room had duplicated the University of Utah's tile floors, the pointy -tipped stainless steel gurneys, and hostile-edged counters and monitors, there would've been multiple and significant injuries; but, with our Love Sacs theme and carpeted floors, there was no inappropriate black and blue and there was no blood.

An intravenous line creates an unacceptable condition in two major ways: first, it sets up the conditions for untoward events, probably by way of those swirling concentration gradients mentioned earlier dumping their chemicals directly into the vein before slamming into downstream organs; second, the IV line's simple presence on that NFL player would have added to that innocent shoulder role, a tangled, leaky, bloody mass of tubing tangled up with the medical furniture and equipment that he would've been smashing into.

Many depression sufferers and even more anxiety sufferers (anxiety often requires a higher ketamine dose for effect than does simple depression), benefit from higher doses. But few IV ketamine practitioners venture into the higher intramuscular dose ranges that we utilize for fear, justifiably, of these wild emergence reactions.

In our clinic, limited to intramuscular injection, the local world is entirely different from the "operating room environment" of the University. Love sacs, carpets, and soft corners dominate. Plus, when patients have demonstrated a propensity for emergence reaction, we set up "restraint areas" where the patient enjoys a "padded room" where he is very much protected from hurting himself.

This is an evolving concept; the formal rules guiding the use of patient restraint must be respected, so we are doing creative things like padding corner walls and placing a love sac in that corner in such a way that the patient is protected while at the same time honoring his sense of freedom and respect.

These emergence reactions, then, take on an entirely different persona when predictable and relatively controllable. Different terms are probably more applicable. "Ego-death" is one of the terms from Buddhism that we apply to a ketamine-induced state of confusion and fear.

These ego-deaths usually last less than 10 minutes and are, then, eminently containable. But with an intravenous line threatening to increase the rate of untoward events, rip flesh, spray blood, and generally defy protocol safety, it's no wonder those practitioners avoid higher doses.

The Great Divider: The Real Cost of the High Cost of an IV.

Intravenous ketamine always costs more than IM ketamine. Why? It's not the cost of the IV. The drug itself costs only a dollar or two per dose, and the IV maybe $10 more, but $500-$1200 per infusion is the norm. This translates to as much as $30,000 a year.

Howard Schultz quotes the Federal Reserve as saying that only 50% of America can get together $400. My $300 per dose price suggests that, for half of America, *my clinic is the only financially available option for ketamine.* If I do a little math on my $300, a local anesthesiology clinic's $1200 (the most expensive guys in town), and use the figure of 80 million for the population in dire need of ketamine, I can assert that for every dollar over the price of my $300/dose of ketamine, *you deny 100,000 Americans access to ketamine.*

And depression is undeniably a life and death disease. This means that when promoting treatment designs that do not maximize treated individuals, there is at least a little bit of redrum in the Kool-Aid being served. Statistical murder still results in real people dying and real death occurring as a product of decision-making. Not treating the maximal number of patients possible in a life-and-death situation will, by definition, always result in some measure of increased dying.

How many of the depressed are being reached by ketamine? Certainly less than 1%. With this current situation of wealth inequality and restricted access to healthcare, only a few folks with spare cash have the opportunity of properly addressing their pathologic lateral habenular burst mode.

Never have so many thoroughly sick people been
so thoroughly ignored by their fellows who are so
thoroughly capable of treating them.

America is seeing a growing epidemic of depression, anxiety and PTSD focused most intensely on the iGens, the 12-20-year-old kids who are currently being savaged by the smart phone and Mr. Zuckerberg's Facebook. We ought to be treating this as the incredibly dangerous epidemic that it is, rather than suppressing the single most valuable antidepressant the world has ever seen at a time when depression and anxiety threaten our society, our nation, and the planet itself.

The intravenous utilization of ketamine should be limited to the operating room and other clinical situations where genuine procedural conscious sedation is been implemented with specific procedural goals in mind.

The application of ketamine to depression, on the other hand, is most safely offered through the intramuscular route. The intramuscular route is also potentially fundamentally cheaper, which save lives in the grand national scheme of addressing this growing epidemic of individual despair and national confusion.

But as I assert IM over IV, I also assert the ketamine troche to be generally superior to any parenteral route, though with the troche we seldom reach that most hallowed goal of a lengthy interval of freedom from depression lasting as long as 2-3 months.

CHAPTER 15

The Five Practical Concerns of Low-dose Ketamine for Depression

There are five practical concerns that must be considered whenever administering low-dose ketamine. They are:

1. The fall risk.
2. Nausea and vomiting.
3. Elevated blood pressure.
4. Elevated liver enzymes.
5. The "freak-out" or emergence reaction.

The Fall Risk

Low-dose ketamine is an extremely safe drug. The single most dangerous aspect of ketamine is prompted by going to the bathroom. That "most dangerous" status we confer on the fall-risk induced by ketamine. The adverse events discussed in a different chapter all have as extremes the possibility for placing the patient in a life-and-death situation. But the likelihood of those events occurring are exceedingly low, especially with the intramuscular route, leaving the very genuine risk of falling and its consequent injuries as the single most dangerous threat of low-dose ketamine.

Though intramuscular ketamine is less likely to induce dangerous adverse events than the intravenous route, that increased safety allows higher dosages which in turn increase the likelihood and frequency of emergence reactions which means that the fall risk with intramuscular ketamine must be dealt with in an expectant and comprehensive mode.

Our stepped system for administering ketamine both results in larger total doses of ketamine as well as longer periods of actual psychedelic experience. Both aspects of ketamine treatment increase the fall-risk exposure.

This is an ongoing area of concern and improvement without a completely satisfying answer. When needed, we utilize distant video observation, pressure-operated alarms, and special padded areas for patients that have demonstrated high likelihood of "psychedelic behavior violations."

None have proven totally satisfactory; "ketamine drunkenness," if allowed full expression, will eventually result in injurious falls. Countermeasures help; in over 7000 treatments, we have yet to experience a patient injury from a fall suffered at our facility. But we will.

The gold standard of addressing the fall risk of ketamine therapy is a constantly attendant chaperone. This means not just the hallways but also into the bathroom. Beyond exotic circus-type suspension devices yet-to-be-developed, a helpful neighbor is the most certain pathway of non-injury into and out of the bathroom

Our consent form acknowledges this frustrating vulnerability and asks the patient to understand and accept this necessary risk as a part of the ketamine treatment.

Nausea and Vomiting

Nausea frequently accompanies ketamine; probably on the order of one in three patients will suffer this discomfort. And unlike other nauseas, ketamine's nausea has a unique potential for morbidity and mortality that simply doesn't exist in other medical situations.

In the past 40 years of emergency medicine, I've seen tens of thousands of nausea-afflicted patients, and not one of these episodes of nausea would I deem dangerous. They were certainly uncomfortable and unliked, but their threat was limited to some measure of discomfort. Death simply wasn't a potential consequence of the nausea.

But depression is a potentially life-threatening disease. And ketamine, as we are arguing, may have unique access to improving any patient's depression. In a patient suffering suicidal ideation, successfully addressing that nausea could save a life or, at the very least, increase the happiness of a life well-lived in contrast to one riven with depression.

So, dealing with the nausea in this situation is especially valuable.

In general, pretreatment of nausea is far preferable to playing "catch-up." We will certainly administer Zofran and/or Phenergan to patients suffering nausea, but having patients demonstrably vulnerable to ketamine's nausea pretreat from home is vastly preferable.

Nausea that penetrates a pretreatment with Zofran, might very likely respond to a regimen of oral Phenergan the preceding night followed by that same Zofran an hour before the ketamine.

One more level of treatment might include a scopolamine skin patch the night before.

Hypertension

Most patients have some measure of elevated diastolic and systolic blood pressure when exposed to ketamine. Usually this is approximately what one might expect from increases during athletic or sexual activities, namely in the 20-50% range of elevation for both diastolic and systolic blood pressures. These elevations we consider acceptable, and seeing them as products of ketamine when starting from a normal blood pressure would generally be considered normal for the situation.

But, elevations beyond these approximate ranges, are not acceptable. Also, resting blood pressures above standard, protocol- defined values must also be defined as unacceptable and require at least evaluation before ketamine treatment, and may dictate actual exclusion.

For minimally elevated blood pressures, I may treat with clonidine and/or Ativan, but for higher levels I very often require a series of blood pressures taken at home and logged in a journal. If those home blood pressures are satisfactorily low, I may define the patient as a "white coat syndrome" and continue treatment. If they are high, however, the patient requires treatment for his hypertension by his treating physician. He may then return to the clinic for ketamine to address his depression.

And for patients passing designated triggers during the treatment, I may offer clonidine and/or Ativan. This would, of course, also move the patient closer to a required hypertension evaluation by his private physician.

Please see the chapter entitled "Clinical Treatment Protocols" for further elucidation.

Elevated Liver Enzymes

This is a concern with little definition. Much like people who enjoy daily wine, a nonspecific, low-level elevation of liver enzymes is sometimes seen. If ketamine treatment is continued, a periodic chemistry panel to evaluate your liver is recommended.

With a history of liver problems, an initial baseline chemistry with periodic repeats might be indicated.

Bad Trips, Freak-outs and Emergence Reactions.

The best part of a ketamine "freak-out," or emergence reaction, comes from its half-life of 20 minutes, which means that the longest that the physiology of a "bad trip" on ketamine might last is 10 minutes. This is certainly a subjective improvement over the 10 hours of bad trip that might conceivably follow an LSD ingestion.

In very general terms, we can place ketamine's convergence reactions in one of two categories: panic attacks and "getting lost in a loop of infinity where you think you aren't coming back." The first of these is an experience suffered often by many people and witnessed by many more; the second is the much-feared and much talked about variety that has rightfully plagued the psychedelic experience since the "Flower Children" years.

Panic attacks represent usually short periods of anxiety where escape is sought through the experience that accompanies a lowering of respiratory CO2 and the physiologic changes that follow. They can be induced by local stressors in the environment or by more drawn out, internal stressors which can induce virtually any level of chronicity.

In the ketamine situation, we can also suggest the possibility that the drug itself is playing a role in the hyperventilation in that ketamine is the only drug known to actually stimulate and preserve respiration even into the anesthetic state. This is a thought of mostly academic rather than practical interest.

The appropriate response to a panic attack induced by ketamine is to, first of all, withhold anymore ketamine for the day. Talking the patient down in a soothing, reassuring voice is certainly appropriate, as is directing him to breathe more slowly, but the patient seldom listens adequately. After all, they are both anxious in the mode of any normal panic attack, plus this panic attack has ketamine as an additive.

So, even though they don't listen to you giving your expert, earnest and sympathetic advice, their breathing returns to normal after the 10 minutes dictated by the half-life of ketamine. Giving more ketamine after a panic attack has a very high likelihood of rejuvenating the attack, so I don't do it. If anxiety remains high, I may consider giving a dose of Ativan. Most of my attention is directed toward assuring the patient that this particular response can be altered and redirected. I've had much success with a protocol approach of discharging the patient to administer the same dose 1 to 2 days later, possibly with Ativan if I believe that anxiety is playing a dominant role. Usually, the patient returns to be given the same dose and does not suffer the panic attack.

The second type of freak out is a true freak out, but has characteristics that completely alter our fears of it. I call this response "Getting lost in a loop of infinity," because the patient is truly consumed by storied dreams of total involvement where return to the normalcy of the clinic is not a seeming option. Two characteristics of this phenomena stand out: 1). The patient remembers nothing of the events; 2). The next day is experienced as one of major happiness, *as though some important mental conflict had been resolved.*

This situation I usually illustrate with a specific patient event. Following a moderate dose of IM ketamine, I once had an NFL defense end more cut than Lebron rolling around an office treatment room while confused and frightened. He did this for an interminable five minutes. I normally point out the horror show that would've transpired had he had an IV in place, but now we are here to note the two facts predicted above: he had no memory of the event, (I did what?) and the next day he started looking back on as *the happiest day of his life.*

Not all freak outs are this positive, but enough are of this variety to warrant seriously asking the question, "Wouldn't you *rather* have a freak-out event?" If you don't remember it, and you know it made you happy, of course you would choose to "kiss the beast of freak-out."

My protocol approach to this second variety of convergence reaction is similar to the first. No more ketamine for the day, then, on their next scheduled return, they get the same dose, *usually to go on with their treatment progress as though nothing negative had happened.*

That is the approach I took with this defensive end. His future treatments did, in fact, turn out to be normal and freak-out free.

CHAPTER 16

Clinical Treatment Protocols and Standing Orders

Key Understandings and Definitions:

Ultimate Goals of Ketamine SLC:

1. To provide maximum depression relief.
2. To define the uniquely appropriate dosage and route of administration for each patient.
3. To provide the cheapest ketamine in America by reducing the established 6-session protocol to a *single ketamine booster every three months.*

All doses are to be administered only after a consenting conversation between the caregiver and the patient.

The half-life of ketamine = 20 minutes for 80% of the activity.

A "leg" = one ketamine intramuscular injection from needlestick through "peak effect" at 18-20 minutes to return to baseline at 30-40 minutes.

"Holy Grail of Depression:" unique to ketamine, this holy Grail amounts to at least three months of freedom from depression, drug levels or drug side effects.

A ketamine "step" = a single ketamine injection or leg in the 11-step series of increasing doses that builds a patient's ketamine tolerance toward a regimen that qualifies for the "Holy Grail of Depression."

1. Each step becomes an identifiable position on the psychedelic ladder between the initial protocol dose of 0.5 mg per kilogram and the target dose for the booster injection of 1.2 mg per kilogram.
2. Each step also provides a valuable opportunity for patient evaluation with respect to such factors as blood pressure, level of nausea and psychedelic intensity.

A "booster" = a collection of 3-6 ketamine legs given 30 minutes apart. After the initial series of stepped ketamine injections, only boosters are administered.

Ketamine Interval = the depression-free period of time between a ketamine booster and the return of his depression.

Dosing for the Initial Two Steps of the 11 Step Ketamine Series named KISSD.

Initial session = diminished, gentle protocol dose plus first progressed dose.

1. Ketamine Protocol Dose = 0.5 mg/kg.
2. Diminished protocol dose = protocol dose minus 5 to 10 mg.
3. First progressed dose = diminished protocol dose plus 5 to 10 mg.
4. increase for a progressed dose equals either 5 mg or 10 mg depending upon the patient's body weight.
    a. If 140 pounds or below, the progressed dosage will generally be 5 mg.
    b. If greater than 140 pounds, the progressed dosage will generally be 10 mg.
    c. These amounts are minimally flexible with each specific patient requirement.

Sessions #2-5.

1. Each session is comprised of two injections 30 minutes apart.
2. Each injection sees a dosage increase of 5 to 10 mg.
3. Target dose = approximately 1.2mg/ kg. = largest dose of the 5th session.

Session #6.

1. First Booster Dose = 3 legs of the largest dose reached during session number 5.
2. This represents the condensation of the conventional ketamine protocol of a series of six treatments into a single treatment of equivalent milligramadge that should qualify the brain of the depressed patient for the "Holy Grail of Depression," namely, three months depression-free status with no drug levels and, consequently, no side effects.

3. The patient will then be released to return to the clinic upon the return of their depression.
    1. Success here is defined as one ketamine booster every 1 to 3 months.
    2. Subsequent ketamine boosters will be manipulated to provide the longest ketamine interval possible.

Ketamine Boosters

Upon return to the clinic with newly returned depression following a series of ketamine treatments, the depression-free interval since the last booster will be the major determinant defining adjustments in treatment. Those adjustments will all be directed towards increasing the depression-free interval.

Anti-nauseants

Agents available:

1. Ondansetron is available PO in 4 mg and 8 mg preparations, and is available for intramuscular usage in flexible dosages, usually of 4 to 8 mg to maximum 16 mg in 8 hours.
2. Phenergan is available in 12.5 and 25 mg preparations, both PO and IM routes only. A "progressed" mode of Phenergan the night before and Zofran one hour before offers a sometimes especially effective regimen.
3. Scopolamine patches are available in 25 mg preparations and must be applied the night before.

Philosophy of administration: approximately one third of ketamine patients will require anti-nauseants and will progress in their requirements during the treatment series. Most medicine additions will be in response to clinical situations, rather than protocol pretreatment. Various combinations of progress in this mode are possible.

Anti-hypertensives

Clonidine is available as a 0.1 mg tablet and may be administered in amounts from 0.1 mg to 0.4 mg within a six hour period.

Specific clinical indications:

Resting pretreatment blood pressure of greater than 140/90.

Ketamine-associated blood pressure elevations of greater than:

1. 200 systolic.
2. 120 diastolic.

White Coat Syndrome:

Addressing the "white coat syndrome," defined as an emotionally-derived elevation of blood pressure not representative of fundamental hypertension.

This presents at the time of administration of the ketamine and confuses the procedure by suggesting a need for antihypertensives where there is, in fact, no need; a white coat syndrome will see no significant elevation of blood pressure during the ketamine, but a person with true baseline hypertension may see his blood pressure elevate into dangerous areas where serious maladies may present.

Once this situation is recognized, the patient may be defined as a white coat syndrome and ketamine may be administered, though a cautious approach should be encouraged. Finding a "cautious approach" is not obvious. One, which I am naming the "Silverstein procedure," after the patient who first enjoyed it, starts with a situation that "looks like" a white coat syndrome (for instance, a recent history of a series of normal blood pressures followed by an elevated, pre-ketamine blood pressure.) This particular cautious approach involved dividing the calculated ketamine dose into four parts and then giving one of them at a time. When I did this the first time, the patient's blood pressure came down a small amount. Repeating the dose did the same again. I did this twice more and the patient had an elevation to a diastolic of 122. I took this to mean that future elevations of ketamine would require an increase in his conventional antihypertensives.

Anxiety

Lorazepam is available in 0.5 mg preparations PO, and as IM injection, usually in 0.5 mg or 1.0 mg administrations.

CHAPTER 17

The Ketamine Consent Form

Overview

Ketamine is a unique medicine that has been used as a general anesthetic and tranquilizer for both animals and humans for the past 50 years. It is described in the FDA literature as a dissociative agent and has been placed pharmacologically in a Schedule III designation. 15 years ago, ketamine was found to be a dramatically effective antidepressant, even in patients that had not responded to other agents. This came at a time when most other frontline antidepressants were being revealed as essentially ineffective in all but the most extreme depressions.

Ketamine is uniquely effective in its rate of response, many seeing near immediate remission of their depression symptoms. Though ketamine's response rate is quite high, there are treatment failures, just as there are significant numbers that relapse over time.

The spectrum of disease addressed by ketamine has grown over the past few years to include not only depression, anxiety and PTSD, but now also includes OCD, reducing by 25 to 50% the symptoms of OCD. And while treating the specific symptoms of OCD, ketamine also coincidentally treats OCD's depression and anxiety.

Though ketamine is a pain medicine while there is a blood level, its half-life limits direct pain control to the short period of its presence. And though that direct pain control is limited, the reduced depression and anxiety effectively *reduces the experience of the chronic pain for a much longer interval.* To be more concrete, we note that the direct pain control of ketamine might be limited to a one to two-hour interval, but the decreased depression might continue for days or weeks afterward with a coincidental decrease in the overall experience of pain during that same period.

Off-label Use:

> Until recently, ketamine was considered off label and therefore did not have a formal indication for treatment of depression, anxiety or any other psychiatric condition. With the FDA approval of Esketamine for the treatment of depression, however, only the most extreme advocates of big Pharma predation would suggest that ketamine, essentially the same molecule but with more antidepressant qualities than those of Esketamine, is effectively off label.

This continued off label designation is really a continuation of the "America is a feedlot to feed upon," practice that has pushed Big Pharma to shun and cloister ketamine in order to protect the billions of dollars brought in by the industry's virtually worthless SSRIs.

This feeding upon its citizens, as is so clearly the case by Big Pharma, has been called the greatest moral failing in the history of mankind, resulting as it does in imposing – for money - the worst disease known to mankind, depression, upon its fellow citizens.

Mechanisms of Action

Ketamine is designated as an NMDA antagonist which blocks the neurotransmitter glutamate. But ketamine has many actions beyond this including:

1. Psychedelia. We have known since medical studies during the Nixon years that LSD and psilocybin give relief from depression, but that relief is partial, short-lived and enjoyed only after the very bulky administration of these demanding and time-consuming psychedelics.
2. Lateral Habenular Burst Mode Abatement. The primary source of depression in most people was revealed for the first time in the February 15, 2018 issue of the world's #1 science journal, *Nature*, in an article which described and defined the lateral habenula as our brain organ of despair. The lateral habenula records every instance of stress, and when the patient passes his own unique tipping point, the lateral habenula sends out the

lateral habenular burst mode, a neurologic code which sends the message to the rest of the brain to, first of all, go into a particular stressed state of mind where that mind is more concerned with looking for Tigers than sniffing flowers. Artificial induction of this mode brings about immediate despair, while the administration of ketamine just as immediately reverses the much feared lateral habenular burst mode and *reverses the despair*. This, specifically, is where ketamine induces its "born-again Christian" level of joy. The opening sentence of this article asserts that ketamine is, "the most important advance in the field of psychiatry in the past half-century." I have yet to meet a psychiatrist that has read this article; this sentence is, I believe, the reason.

3. Dendritic Repair. We have known for a number of years that, in the hippocampus, ketamine's stimulation of the mTOR (mammalian target of rapamycin) pathway resulted in varieties of dendritic repair that was assumed to be responsible for improvements of memory where it had been compromised by depression. Also, recently, NPR reported studies that recognized a two-stage process of dendritic repair in the "stress regions of the brain." Knowing that every neuron of our brain connects to another thousand neurons by way of dendrites, this set of observations suggests that dendritic repair may very well play a foundational role in mental health at least equivalent to the role played by changing the oil of your automobile.
4. And last for this list, is a study at Stanford where the anti-depressant quality of ketamine was blocked by coincident administration of naltrexone, an opiate blocker. This suggests an important association with the body's internal opiate system that may prove to be a valuable focus for searches for new treatments in the future.

Route of Administration

Ketamine enjoys multiple modes of administration each with its own parameters of effect as evidenced in the following table:

Route	Time of Onset	Percentage Absorption
Intravenous	<1 minute	100%
Intramuscular	2 to 3 minutes	97%
Nasal spray	15 to 30 minutes	10%
Oral	<30 minutes	15 to 20%
Sublingual	<15 minutes	30%

The conventional route for parenteral administration has always been intravenous; this is a drug designed for the operating room and, when in the operating room, an IV is always present. And when an IV is present, it is used.

But when not in the operating room, as when treating depression with its requirements for only a fraction of the usual operating room dose, there is much question about the safety of intravenous usage. (Please see the discussion on IV vs IM usage elsewhere in this article for a discussion on that topic.) Combining those difficulties with issues relating to the problems with emergence reactions in this low-dose situation, *virtually precludes proper dosing with intravenous usage.*

The future of ketamine rests in the ketamine troche. Intravenous usage, a product of convention combined with the fetish of anesthesia, will soon give way to intramuscular usage. This will become more obvious during the discussion of our unique step system of ketamine administration, termed "KISSD," for *Ketamine Intramuscular Stepped System for Depression*, elsewhere in this work.

Dosing Protocols

There are a variety of dosing protocols in practice. The original protocol presented by Dr. Krystal at Yale is the starting point for most of them:

0.5 mg/kg given by IV infusion over 40 minutes.

This protocol included six of these minimalist protocol doses over 12 days and promised a three-month interval of freedom from depression during which time no drug level would be seen and, therefore, no side effects would be experienced.

This three-month period of normalcy could, in fact, be termed the "Holy Grail of Ketamine Therapy" because it is just that. This is the apex of depression therapy; NOTHING in medicine rivals it.

But this holy Grail of ketamine therapy seems to have been abandoned across most of the ketamine medical industry. The reason for this altered course from an important goal, I believe, is the awkwardness that most physicians are discovering with their IV approach to ketamine.

Only approximately 2/5 of ketamine patients will go on to enjoy this three-month interval of no depression. Pursuing that goal is more difficult using an IV and is simply unavailable with ketamine troches. This is discussed in much more depth in the third chapter, entitled, "KISSD: The Ketamine Intramuscular Stepped System for Depression."

Effects of Ketamine

The acute subjective experience of ketamine is generally described by pharmacologists as "dissociative," which comes from the conceptualization of a separation of mind and body. The more public term would be psychedelic.

Psychedelics are recognized as being responsible for possibly the most challenging experiences that a conscious mind can know. Few people have not heard stories of "bad trips and freak outs" being told alongside tales describing glorious "spiritual experiences" and "insights into God." Though psychedelics can be challenging, familiarity and ready acceptance come with frequent exposure.

This is the core of our stepped system for depression where acceptance of the medicine is cultivated through a predictably graduated increase in dosage over time. Again, this will be discussed in much more depth in the chapter on KISSD, where much higher doses that are consequently much more therapeutic are cultivated.

Patient response with changes in their depression are hugely variable. A small fraction of patients will find extreme joy and, likewise, a small fraction (about one in 400) will find significant fear and even terror. Much of this can be mitigated by way of the meme of "set and setting," which suggests that much of the psychedelic experience comes from two things: the patient's immediate environment and the brain state he brings to the treatment session. But some of these negative states are simply not predictable, being a product of dark depths present in every mind being released by the creativity and immediate relentlessness of psychedelia.

The specific nature of these varieties of what we call "emergence reactions" is discussed in the section on adverse events.

Ketamine Assisted Psychotherapy

Much is said of the role of psychotherapy in conjunction with any medication, but the world's needs for psychotherapy, in the context of ketamine, have changed hugely. Consider that with SSRIs, the across-the-board percentage response rate is at best in single digits.

This fact, combined with the very significant side effects and undefined, vague mental changes that might best be termed for each, shifting one of them, "Shrink-wrapped twilight zones," both the prescriber of the SSRIs and the therapist have constantly moving and changing targets to deal with. In many ways, the therapist's role is far more important with SSRIs because *the patient never really leaves an unwell state*; she, the therapist, is always needed.

But, with ketamine, the patient returns to a *state of normalcy* a very high percentage of the time. The drug, ketamine, very often removes the depression, the anxiety and the PTSD, or at least makes them much better. The patient's problems now may be more akin to a healthy mental state such as adolescence where, rather than experiencing a transition from childhood to adult, the patient is *moving from depression or anxiety to a state of normalcy.* The patient in this situation needs simple guidance about living life in general: how to carry on a normal conversation or maybe even how to conduct a loving relationship with another human being; how to date; how to exhilarate on a fine spring day. In some measure these everyday experiences are to be relearned. How much of a therapist is needed for such commonplace experiences and opportunities for growth varies hugely with the recently post- depression individual, just as it does in many ways for every high school graduate.

I believe that in this new world of exceedingly treatable stress diseases, the getting of the ketamine is *by far the most important part of any successful treatment.* And, to back up that sentiment in the harshest of terms, I present the simple fact that there *aren't enough therapists to deliver adequate care to all those 80 million in need.*

Ketamine clinics will play the major role in liberating America from whatever monster or set of circumstances is responsible for this nationwide epidemic of anxiety, depression, PTSD and despair, while therapists will certainly rush in to hold their hands, often with positive effect.

Medical Clearance for Treatment

Before ketamine treatment, overall health should be assessed by one's primary care provider, with special attention to respiratory and cardiovascular status. Basic chemistries and urinalysis should be attended to. If indicated, an EKG should be performed.

Exclusion from ketamine therapy would be indicated with a history of a recent MI, certain dysrhythmias, narrow angle glaucoma, hyperthyroidism or any unstable medical conditions such as uncontrolled hypertension or pulmonary disease. With any questions, referral to appropriate specialists is indicated. Except for antihypertensives and sedatives, the patient's mental health meds are best held on the day of treatment. For Lamictal and Wellbutrin, I suggest that the patient hold them for a full 24 hours prior to receiving ketamine.

A general drug screen can reveal certain vulnerabilities and can direct the caregiver to appropriate treatment directives. Opiates pose a unique risk in that an antidepressant dose can return an addict to

virgin status, putting that addict at significant risk if he returns to his conventional opiate dosage after a ketamine treatment.

Adverse and Side Effects Associated with Ketamine Treatment

1. First, a list of common, to-be-expected symptoms of ketamine administration:
    a. A sense of acute loss of control, as though consciousness were being "grabbed" by some "force." "Relax," would be the seldom listened-to exhortation.
    b. Nausea, vomiting.
    c. Impaired coordination.

d. Restlessness.
e. Headache.
f. Blurred vision.
g. Confusion

2. The single most dangerous aspect of ketamine treatment is going to the bathroom. There is a significant fall risk from ketamine that is hugely enhanced by the high likelihood of emergence reactions combined with the inevitability of having to use the restroom. Both situations require chaperones to address these needs. We have experimented with alarms and constant video, but *only another adequately sized individual provides the necessary safety*, and even then, there is risk.
3. Ketamine increases sympathetic tone in the vasculature and predictably raises both systolic and diastolic blood pressure 10 to 50%. This must be addressed in a protocol fashion with appropriate triggers for antihypertensives and sedatives as needed.
4. One patient in three will suffer nausea and related consequences. Attention to appropriate food restrictions, namely nothing by mouth for the four hours preceding the ketamine, is key. Some caregivers pretreat every patient. Whether or not that is done, progression in the use of anti- nauseants is extremely common. I usually wait until the first instance of nausea, and then titrate medicines to the nausea. Knowing that the likelihood of nausea will only increase with increased ketamine dosage, I will phone in a prescription for both Zofran and Phenergan that in the future will allow a progressed approach to their nausea.
5. Cystitis is a problem more of the street than of clinical usage. In 2,000 patients, I have yet to see a single complaint of cystitis attributable to the ketamine.
6. Liver enzyme elevation is reported to occur in a small percentage of patients. In addition to the baseline chemistries suggested above for general screening, I will generally repeat those chemistries after six months to a year of ketamine treatment to assess changes.
7. Glottic spasm and apnea are listed in the insert and certainly occur in the operating room environment. I have

seen one patient with apnea; she responded with normal respirations with a shake of her shoulder, but it was a genuinely dangerous event. This occurred during IV administration of ketamine. I have not seen a similar instance with intramuscular usage and have heard no reports of glottic spasm during intramuscular or ketamine troche usage.

8. Though ketamine does have a risk of abuse, it has no physiologic withdrawal syndrome such as that seen with opiates or benzodiazepines. We see a very small percentage of patients who seem to forever crave a larger dose, some without apparent ill effect. These must be evaluated individually, probably with benefits from referral to specialists.
9. There is talk of bipolar patients with a manic component suffering from ketamine. I have been unable to find instances in the literature of this phenomena, and I have treated many bipolar patients that carry a diagnosis of mania with ketamine with no adverse events or consequence other than happy outcomes.
10. Bad Trips, Freak Outs and Other Emergence Reactions are varied frights of psychedelia that frighten the responsible physician as much as the patient, and constrain and confuse the environment of administration as much as they limit dosages, consequent treatment success and the reach of ketamine to the population in need of it. KISSD, our stepped system of ketamine administration addresses these ugly stepchildren of the promise of ketamine psychedelia by embracing them, adapting to them, and then utilizing the consequent higher dosages for improved effectiveness and rate of "cure." These bizarre, defining events will be given the entire next chapter.

Management of Adverse Effects:

In over 8000 treatments, we have never utilized our crash cart and don't expect to. We commonly utilize sedatives, anti-nauseants, and the occasional antihypertensive. CPR is an option, and we do have AEDs and the medical tools to manage airways. A crash cart is present, but I have never utilized it and do not anticipate confronting a situation where it will be required.

Most of the genuinely important actions, however, are preemptive and consist of having chaperone-caregivers always ready to help patients while in the clinic or on the way to their car with a shoulder to lean on or a wheelchair to sit in.

Very occasionally a medical situation will present that requires further evaluation or even a higher level of care. If the judgment of the treating provider suggests that either situation pertains, the EMS system may be activated to transport the patient to a different facility.

Patient Preparation for Ketamine Treatment

1. Patients should abstain from all substance use for at least 48 hours; this includes tobacco, alcohol, cannabis and all illicit substances.
2. On the day of first treatment, a urine toxicology screen will be performed.
3. No intake by mouth, other than small sips of water, for the four hours prior to treatment.
4. In addition to the above-mentioned admonition against substance use, any stimulant medication that might raise blood pressure should also be held.
5. Diabetes and hypertension medications should be continued, with insulin adjusted to meet the nothing-by- mouth requirement.

The Ketamine Treatment Experience

Check-in and Preparation

1. On the first day, there will be varieties of set up for the coming months of ketamine treatment. This will involve data acquisition that includes past medical records, a viewing of the ketamine videos as a part of the general consent, urine toxicology, taking of vital signs, initiation of the MoodMonitor program, examination and history-taking by the caregiver for entrance into the EHR, calculation of the initial dose and, finally, placement of the CareTaker monitoring system.
2. This will also involve evaluation of vital signs and possibly addressing ongoing needs for medications to be added to the

basic ketamine treatment program. On this first day, this may take between one and two hours. On subsequent treatment sessions it will shorten to 10 or 15 minutes.

The Psychedelic Experience

The intramuscular injection of ketamine results in an experience that peaks at approximately 18 minutes and is significantly approaching relative normalcy by 35 to 40 minutes. The blood level reflects this experience with the very first "twinkle" of psychedelia appearing at 2 to 3 minutes, then steadily building to a peak experience over the next 15 to 20 minutes. The following 20 minutes of descent are experienced as a "decreasing psychedelia" to near normalcy.

To describe psychedelia many metaphors of frustration have been utilized, such as describing an abstract painting to a blind person; it is true, and will remain true, that no one understands the psychedelic experience until they've had it. That which is psychedelic can be as scary as scary can be, just as it can be as beautiful as beautiful can be, and as spiritual as spiritual can be. It lights up your 100 billion neurons and excites 5 million years of fantasies, fears and dreams that evolution has seared into the submerged museum-storehouse of your deeper consciousness.

Proper psychologic preparation for ketamine requires that ANYONE presenting for ketamine treatment MUST be prepared to accept potential negative experiences relating to the psychedelic that is ketamine. Frightening memories, created terrors, or conjured social disgraces are all possible creations of any human mind; their potential to present themselves into your consciousness is always a possibility while under the influence of any psychedelic.

Whereas the "bad trips" discussed earlier in this paper are seen as integral and necessary possibilities that flow from any psychedelic experience, the "essence" of the psychedelic experience is being recognized by caregivers more and more as a necessary component of ketamine's healing potential.

Disengagement from Treatment

1. Patients will have agreed to establish an aftercare support person to accompany them for the four hours following treatment.

2. Patients may, of course, stop treatment at any time.
3. They will still be under the medical constraints that address vulnerabilities that accompany the ketamine experience.
4. They will not be allowed to leave the clinic until a certain level of ambulatory facility has been reached, and they will not be allowed to leave the office alone for a period of four hours.
5. Departure from the clinic will include a formal signing out to a responsible party for the four hours of post ketamine treatment that defines patient vulnerability.

Final Declaration

1. In signing this agreement, I recognize that I have a formal relationship with the clinic Ketamine for Depression Salt Lake City.
2. I understand that my response to ketamine treatment may not be the favorable one that I hope for, and that there are risks associated with this treatment; some of these risks could be permanent, though that is unlikely.
3. Current treatment does not necessarily imply continued treatment.
4. Treatment termination may be instituted by the caregiver for a variety of reasons including but not limited to simply a poor fit, noncompliance with care, concern for diversion, patient behaviors and other risk factors that exceed the tolerance of the caregiver.

The Ketamine Treatment Pledges

1. I have viewed and understand the three ketamine videos detailing the use of ketamine in depression and many of the difficulties that attend its administration.
2. I understand ketamine's propensity to elevate blood pressure and occasionally cause an elevation in liver enzymes; this may require appropriate treatment and periodic exams.
3. I understand that in the event of an emergency I will be transported at my expense to the nearest emergency room by way of the EMS system.
4. I agree to avoid using the local court system to settle any dispute

involving care at this facility and will always give a system of arbitration priority.

5. I understand that to receive treatment I must have someone present at the clinic at the time of discharge to sign for responsibility of care and transportation.
6. I understand that ketamine will enhance my urge to use the restroom. I will do my best to allow the medicine to wear off before moving to use the restroom, and I will do so *only* while escorted.
7. I understand that I must not have any solid food by mouth in the four hours before treatment, and that liquids should be limited to small sips of water.
8. I understand that falls are ketamine's greatest risk and that I will therefore do my best not to stand up during treatment.
9. I understand that pregnancy is an absolute contraindication to ketamine; this includes planning to become pregnant. This establishment does not accept responsibility for your pregnancy while undergoing ketamine treatment. We suggest frequent pregnancy tests if this is in any way a concern.
10. I understand that I may be sharing a room with other patients.
11. I understand that this is a clinic where only ketamine is administered, so that virtually everyone is suffering one of the stress diseases. While sharing rooms, short medical conversations may transpire concerning illnesses. In this situation, we do not feel that hearing those conversations constitutes a HIPAA violation. If you do not agree with this HIPAA exception, *please do not be treated at this facility.*
12. Consent for video to "assure safety and mutually mitigate concern for behavior that may be aversive, intrusive, or experienced as such by the patient in an altered state of awareness, such as a gentle hand placed on the shoulder."
13. This clinic does not supply formal, professional mental health care beyond that of a physician. Consequently, the patient is advised to seek coincident therapy from appropriate caregivers.

CHAPTER 18

The Ketamine Emergence Reaction

Ketamine has proven to be a remarkably safe drug that is also extremely effective in the two general areas of its use, anesthesia and the treatment of the stress diseases, depression, anxiety and PTSD. It has multiple mechanisms of action that lend themselves to varieties of treatment situations, but one phenomenon has special sway in creating treatment challenges, introducing special dangers and producing unique areas of confusion to both the patient and the practitioner supplying the ketamine. That phenomenon is the ketamine emergence reaction.

Our knowledge of the ketamine emergence reaction comes from two very different areas. First, ketamine is a general anesthetic which gave birth to the entity, "emergence reaction," a term which applies to any dysphoria or confusion resulting from a general anesthetic; second is the psychedelia which adds to the anesthesia of ketamine the unique, powerful, creative and infinitely subjective mental states of psychedelia.

Many terms and much confusion exist in both the professional and lay communities regarding exactly what these varieties of subjective mental states mean. What exactly are the altered correlates of consciousness of a propofol emergence reaction and how would that differ from ketamine anesthesia? Consider the following terms, all of which refer to varieties of anesthetic and/or psychedelic response:

Emergence reaction or phenomenon.
Emergence delirium.
Ketamine emergence reaction.
Ketamine emergence delirium.
K-hole.
Freak out.
Bad trip.
Ego death.

We will first discuss each term, then we will try to relate that term to how it is applied to ketamine and its use to treat depression, anxiety and PTSD, paying special attention to how its influence may compromise care.

Emergence Reaction or Phenomenon:

The term, "emergence reaction," originated over 50 years ago in the world of anesthesia and was used then to refer to mostly negative moods that would now be more appropriately referred to as delirium. Consequently, I will use the term emergence reaction to include any altered consciousness that is produced by anesthesia or ketamine in lower doses where formal anesthesia is not the product. As such, the term can include neutral or euphoric experiences.

This variety of moods is well expressed in an Australian study published in an emergency medicine journal that examined 745 episodes of ketamine anesthesia to determine that 12.5% of children cried on awakening, 39% experienced pleasant altered perceptions and 2.1% experienced "emergence delirium."

With our restriction of the term "emergence reaction" to non-dysphoric entities, only reactions in the 39% category would be termed emergence reactions.

Emergence Delirium

In Nishan Goudsouzian's 2009 book *A Practice of Anesthesia for Infants and Children,* he related, "ED (emergence delirium) is not a new phenomenon; it was first reported in 1961 and has been reported repeatedly after the introduction of almost every new anesthetic including most inhalation anesthetics as well as IV agents including midazolam, remifentanil, and propofol. The incidence of ED after inhalational anesthesia in children ranges from 2 to 80%.

These altered brain states are always of great concern and have been well studied but their origins remain unclear. Many possibilities have been called upon and include various metabolic alterations such as global changes in lactate or metabolite fluctuation in the parietal lobe, and EEGs have found suggestive correlates looking at the frontal lobe and the locus coeruleus in particular, but no consistent consensus has emerged.

Ketamine Emergence Reaction

Where the original term, "emergence reaction," was a negative experience as discussed above, the possibilities for ketamine are very different. The euphoria of a ketamine treatment would be included in the definition of a ketamine emergence reaction.

This interpretation ambivalence is well expressed in a colorful article from the journal "Anesthesiology," by Craig W. Platt, PhD., in which he describes psychedelic distortions and colors that could be the envy of any psychonaut, but he concludes that the experience was not pleasant and was therefore a delirium.

Is this an example of one man's paradise is another's Hell? I think so.

Ketamine Emergence Delirium

If we had together the above description of emergence delirium and then add a layer of psychedelia to that experience, we can manufacture a definition for this entity, but it says nothing about our understanding the difference. After all, this is a subjective experience to which we have no access. The only way that we can truly access this information is by the taking of ketamine along with the assumption that one's own experience will be like another's, again a highly questionable assumption.

The truth is that we can only observe what is going on with the patient from the outside.

From the outside we can come to some very significant truths. As mentioned earlier in the chapter on adverse events, the best part of a ketamine "bad trip" or "freak out," comes from its 20-minute half-life. This 20-minute half-life means that a bad trip will last only 10 minutes and, in general, this is true, though some feelings can certainly persist longer and, in the case of severe fright, that fright may continue and could reasonably evolve into a PTSD experience.

These bad trips and freak outs can be categorized into two general categories. The first is a simple panic attack driven by hyperventilation where the emotionality of the experience is largely driven by alterations in carbon dioxide and the consequences of electrolyte fluctuations that follow the acid-base changes induced by the lowering carbon dioxide levels. Treatment of hyperventilation is usually a thing of medical protocol but, with the 20-minute half-life of ketamine, the hyperventilation syndrome will usually end spontaneously as a consequence of the dropping ketamine level.

The second variety of ketamine-induced delirium is what I would term, "getting lost in a piece of infinity." This is a genuinely frightening experience where the patient is truly lost in a scenario of his own fantastic construction where he thinks he is not coming back to this world. This would seem to be a horror that would end all future thought of ketamine as an agent of healing, but not so.

Two quite counterintuitive experiences await this patient lost in his ketamine delirium. Whatever physical events or psychologic horrors occurred during the dreams of the delirium, the patient quite simply loses all memory of them. "I did what?" is my favorite question that patients emerging from the scenario might ask. They truly don't remember those frights.

The second counterintuitive experience of a ketamine delirium promises that, for whatever reason, the next day of their life will be *a very happy one, if not the happiest in their life.* This is a high- percentage event.

My formula for dealing with these dysphoric events is to discontinue any further ketamine with the assumption that the patient's "set and setting" is not appropriate for a happy, productive treatment session. I will consider lorazepam as we negotiate a reduction in the dysphoria. When the patient returns in two days for the continuation of his care, I will give *the same or minimally reduced dose*, possibly with Ativan, and usually find that the negative events seldom repeat themselves. If they do, a trial with a different route of administration is in order.

So, do these two counterintuitive experiences of forgotten horror and transformed memory remove the "freak" from freak out? If you don't remember what happened and happiness is your only consequence of the event, don't you want another one?

If only the trip of "bad trip" remains, of course you do.

K-hole

The word "K-hole" comes from the street and originally described a lengthy, confused, horror-filled episode of psychedelia following a ketamine binge. It would commonly be associated with other drugs, malnutrition and varieties of social circumstance.

The word is now used in the ketamine depression clinic setting to describe any "deep" or "disturbing" ketamine experience.

Freak-outs, Bad Trips, and Ego Deaths.

These three terms, the first two coming from the hippie years of the 60's, have subtle differences. The first two are born of American culture and the street, while the last, ego death, is a term from Buddhism that originally alluded to the process of removing a specific roadblock on the road to enlightenment.

In the current world of therapeutic ketamine, ego death has come to refer to a psychedelic experience where the psychonaut gains some special insight into the experience of death itself.

CHAPTER 19

Ketamine Nasal Spray, Troches, and Esketamine

We've discussed the beginnings of ketamine in the operating room where it was always administered intravenously at doses meant for general anesthesia that were 100 times the dose of that required for the treatment of depression anxiety or PTSD. Safer, far more flexible, and allowing of larger doses with their coincidently higher treatment effects, intramuscular usage allows the development of treatment progressions such as KISSD - Ketamine Intramuscular Stepped System for Depression - that present dosage regimens that can be administered in a day to last the three or more months that define what we term "the Holy Grail of Depression."

But, unfortunately, only 40% of patients given this regimen reach that holy Grail. Why? They simply don't have the "perfect brain" required. That is, they suffer the brain maladies termed bipolar, OCD, pain-based, autistic or some other yet undefined entity. The off-the- cuff shared mental component that denies this healing is excess stress produced as a consequence of the innate structure of the brain and its constituent cells that together produce those diseases.

The consequence in KISSD terms is that parenteral ketamine loses much of its appeal, even though it is still inducing healing. Where the intensity and demands of the parenteral ketamine experience are acceptable when they are separated by an interval of 3-4 months, an interval of 1-2 weeks might seem emotionally relentless while its cost is multiplying. Another approach then gains priority, ketamine troches; these tools – the future of ketamine - became available to most of us only in the last two years.

A ketamine troche is a flavored lozenge that is intended to dissolve and be at least partially absorbed under the tongue or in the cheek. It enjoys a 30% absorption rate and comes in doses ranging from 50 mg to 600 mg. It is absorbed in the mouth over 10 to 20 minutes and produces a significant psychedelic experience at the higher doses. It is normally taken every day or every other day in the evening. A chaperone is required at the higher doses, and the medicine may be broken off in pieces to be distributed through the day; this approach is commonly taken as a component of pain control.

The troches are supplied by compounding pharmacies at currently only a few locations where they are formulated, manufactured and then mailed to the patient. Pharmacists have been extremely helpful at both of the local facilities in providing patient instruction and advice.

The ketamine troche experience is quite different from the in clinic parenteral session offered in the physician's presence. When taken at home in that most comfortable of environments, many different offerings and opportunities are available. Meditation and mindfulness are both greatly aided by this situation of comfort. Interpersonal relations are especially susceptible to psychedelic experience in general and ketamine in particular.

The practical experience of ketamine troches begins at a low dose, usually 50 mg troches are prescribed for daily use over a one-month period. This dosage is almost certainly below the eventual therapeutic target dose. The patient can be flexible with this first month dosage, carefully increasing the dosage for a few days and assessing the changes before continuing with another increase.

At higher doses, approximately 300 mg or more, a treatment assessment is in order to determine any problems with changes in vital signs. Blood pressure, O2 sat and pulse are assessed along with the patient's anesthetic response. If the patient does well with this office dose, she is allowed to administer that dose at home with a chaperone present, and is expected to continue the treatment admonitions given in the clinic; no food for the four hours prior to treatment, care with any ambulation, especially to the bathroom where the chaperone should be in attendance, and general attention to "set and setting".

The chaperone's obligation includes monitoring the patient, of course, but also should include a dated log of the events of care which ought to include at least an occasional vital sign.

During this time the patient will be evaluated both verbally and by the Mood Monitor system of PHQ-9 assessments. Periodic assessment is always necessary.

Coincident mental health therapy is much dependent upon the

patient's general response to treatment. As discussed elsewhere in this book, the launching pad for therapy is very different following ketamine where the patient has often been returned to relative normalcy as compared to the sequential creations of conventional mental health care that I term "Shrink-wrapped Twilight Zones."

Personal growth organizations such as the local "Impact" organization have offerings that may very well translate effectively to ketamine programs. We are investigating this now.

In the meantime, the most basic therapy of questing human interaction is always on the agenda for appropriate post-ketamine activity.

CHAPTER 20

Ketamine Pumps and Comas

Currently, the path of ketamine that has as its intention the treatment of depression, anxiety and PTSD, ends with one of three possibilities: 1) an extended period of freedom from depression that we term the "Holy Grail of Depression,"2) daily or near-daily ketamine troches, or 3) treatment failure.

The practical ketamine story currently ends with these possibilities, but there are still options remaining.

Some of these options are waiting on technology to provide tools of administration. My favorite - a programmable, refillable implanted pump - would dole out exactly the right dose at appropriate times of the day. Most of the time the dosing schedule would take place at night during sleep, but experimentation with the drug will yield improved results from mechanisms that we do not yet understand. For instance, will ketamine micro-dosing provide significant advantages, if any, over regular dosing?

An implant pump capable of flexible dosing as described above would be a wonder tool that is almost certain to occur; we will all want one and will enjoy its benefits. Virtually all medicines could be administered through a machine of this sort. I predict its routine presence within 20 years.

The above described implant will give routine and flexible doses at nonstandard times. A ketamine coma promises improved treatment response through the sledgehammer of massive and/or persistent dosing; it seems to work. Its incredible ICU-level expense precludes its routine use, but extreme pain situations, such as that of phantom limb, have responded to this piledriver approach to care.

Currently, the local University is carrying on a treatment for depression that involves 10 sequential propofol comas. I have heard good anecdotal reports on patient response. My first thoughts on this possibility go immediately to Michael Jackson and his non-redoable experience with propofol. The death-risk portion of Michael's response can be obviated, but it cannot be totally excluded. And the cost of general anesthesia...? Certainly far more than could ever be utilized to address the depressed masses of America or the world.

A ketamine coma, on the other hand, is simply not that dangerous. There is not much difference between treating that Vietnam war soldier in the field and a full-on ketamine coma. They are, in fact, the same; only the situations and goals differ.

So why propofol comas at the University and not ketamine comas? Propofol is still under patent. Ketamine is not.

Money clearly matters more than the medicine and the care it renders.

CHAPTER 21

Dogs, Love Sacs, and the Ketamine Aesthetic

In the opening pages of his revelatory book, *How to Change Your Mind,* Michael Pollan muses on the dangers of psychedelics: "But when I began to weigh the potential benefits I was hearing about against the risks, I was surprised to learn that psychedelics are far more frightening to people than they are dangerous. Many of the most notorious perils are either exaggerated or mythical. It is virtually impossible to die from an overdose of LSD or psilocybin, for example, and neither drug is addictive. After trying them once, animals will not seek a second dose, and repeated use by people robs the drugs of their effect."

Timothy Leary is credited with inventing the term "set and setting" to refer respectively to the mental state of the moment, the "set," becoming melded to the physical surroundings, the "setting," to combine in the psychedelic moment to create a particular and unique instance of conscious experience. This conscious experience is exceedingly emotional, powerful and infinitely subjective. It is this fundamental, shifting subjectivity that responds to any stimulus in the environment with wild unpredictability that calls upon attention to set and setting to ensure a productive and pleasant psychedelic experience.

This apex subjectivity is inherent to, and respectful of, what the UCLA psychiatrist Charles Grob called, "the critical extra-pharmacological variables," and what every LSD-imbibing hippie new as a fundamental truth: "You don't go into a supermarket stoned."

The infinite subjectivity of psychedelics is a scientific, medical truth which must be recognized and respected if the benefits of the medicine are to be fully utilized in a maximally safe fashion, which is always the goal of any caregiver of integrity.

Psychedelics carry a taint of rebellion and illegality from the Nixon years which is still affecting authorities overseeing ketamine today. This negativity toward ketamine, born of a nostalgia for hippie-bashing, is as out of place in our times as it is medically harmful to the growing epidemic of depression, anxiety and despair that we are all witnessing on a daily basis.

Catering to the psychedelically altered minds of patients suffering the worst disease known to mankind, depression, is the responsibility of everyone sharing the society. For a lawman to interfere with ketamine treatment for any of these outmoded and inappropriate imperatives is an outrage to which all citizens should respond with fury.

For a pharmaceutical company to constrain the antidepression wonder that is ketamine for moneyed purposes, as is currently the practice in America, the label, "*Perpetrator of the single greatest moral failing in the history of mankind*," must be applied and worn with appropriate disgrace.

CHAPTER 22

The Meaning of Anesthesia with Ketamine at X-depression Doses

Ketamine is classified as a schedule III general anesthetic. As such, its pharmacologic role is defined and restricted to varieties of anesthesia. This is reflected in the dictionary diagnosis of anesthesia.

> Anesthesia: general or local insensibility, as to pain and other sensation, induced by certain interventions or drugs to permit the performance of surgery or other painful procedures.

Two decades ago, however, ketamine was recognized as having great antidepressant qualities. In fact, it is by far the greatest antidepressant known to man and qualifies as a wonder drug that is safe, accessible and cheap. It could be and, in fact, is very likely to be our single greatest answer to the epidemic of depression and anxiety that is besetting our populace, especially our kids.

As quoted from *Nature* magazine multiple times elsewhere in this paper: "The discovery of the rapid antidepressant effects of the NMDAR antagonist ketamine is arguably the most important advance in the field of psychiatry in the past half-century."

This new usage will almost certainly be the mechanism for ketamine's most profound impact on our society. Where previously ketamine's relationship with anesthesia was an obvious one - the patient was either "under anesthesia" or was emerging from it - the nature of a parenteral ketamine treatment for depression "nudges up" against changes in patient consciousness that bring into question whether or not actual anesthesia is being performed.

Normally, this is a very significant question and implies a dynamic relationship with patient risk. Specifically, when a patient approaches what we would call anesthesia as a product of anesthetic induction, his risk markedly increases with all anesthetic agents *except ketamine.*

For instance, if a patient were to be given propofol, a popular general anesthetic, at an appropriate rate and dosage such that the definition of anesthesia were being encroached upon, no anesthesiologist would doubt that that patient was at increased risk for various complications that might threaten death. If the signs of anesthesia were diminished verbal response, lack of attention and drooling, the anesthesiologist would know from these signs that the patient was at risk for aspiration, apnea and hypotension.

The anesthesiologist would know this because the changes in consciousness that produce the diminished verbal response, lack of attention and drooling were *functioning as a vital sign.* As with blood pressure, pulse, respiratory rate and oxygen saturation, *any significant change in a vital sign from normal implies specific dangers that are specific to that vital sign.* If the patient drops their blood pressure or sees it elevate dramatically, there is some measure of trouble that the anesthesiologist must deal with. If respirations drop or elevate, there is this similar set of concerns which must be addressed.

Diminished mentation is a vital sign that portends danger with every general anesthetic known to man *except ketamine.* Diminished mentation as a vital sign also portends danger with opiates, barbiturates and alcohol. Only ketamine discounts changes in mentation as a genuine vital sign.

Why is this?

The answer is simple; ketamine is the only recognized direct stimulant of respirations. The drug became famous for this quality in Vietnam where a soldier in the field in need of a procedure could be administered ketamine, the bullet could be taken out, the wound dressed, and the soldier could then be loaded on a gurney and flown to a higher care facility.

So, when a patient is being treated for depression and the dosage is increased as a part of the care, a patient may have his conscious state creep into what might be called "anesthesia." For instance, the patient may not respond to verbal challenge or even a shaking of the shoulder, and this might be coincident with increased nystagmus and a gaze focused into the distance.

If respirations and O2-sat are normal along with blood pressure and pulse, is this patient in "anesthesia?" And if we determine that he is indeed anesthetic, do we care? And if so, why do we care?

By definition, the patient is demonstrating "general or local insensibility to pain as induced by a drug," satisfying the dictionary portrait of anesthesia. But does this set of observations qualify as a vital sign which would then mean that that set of observations is then predictive of valid dangers that should be addressed in order to preserve the health or well-being of the patient?

The answer I have is, quite simply and definitively, no. The "anesthesia" that we've just defined by way of the dictionary does not help us improve the quality of health or decrease the exposed danger for the patient when we are speaking of ketamine.

But there is a role in a ketamine for depression clinic for observing that anesthetic status. As with the KISSD step system for treating depression with ketamine, each step represents a psychological level of psychedelia that serves as a reference point for both the patient and the caregiver. When a step of this system is defined as being anesthetic, we back off and give a lower dose *simply because we've reached a reference point*. This reference point, we've discovered through the trial and error of thousands of ketamine treatments, occurs around the dosage of 1.2 mg per kilogram given as an intramuscular injection.

At doses higher than 1.2 mg per kilogram, we've noticed an increased rate of emergence phenomena; this is the primary reason for respecting anesthesia as a vital sign. Also, local authorities not readily conversant in the terms or the concepts of anesthesia, especially as it applies to ketamine as an exception, are directed by conventional authorities to be especially wary of situations involving anesthesia. This is, of course, as it should be; anesthesia and procedural consciousness are areas of much morbidity and mortality.

Ketamine for Depression Salt Lake City considers itself especially sensitive to this layered situation. Utilizing the industry-leading CareTaker monitoring system, and employing constant-care, one-on-one chaperones, we have a system for dealing with the ketamine emergence reaction.

With close to 8000 treatments ketamine SLC has yet to suffer a significant injury from fall or a medical problem associated with the KISSD stepped system of ketamine administration.

We believe this ketamine system to be a depression-hungry eagle filled with promise as it circles the heights above.

CHAPTER 23

Ketamine Prophecy and the Humanism of Sir William Osler

At this moment the forces of Big Pharma in America are focused on ketamine's role in the mental health world with more intensity and moneyed intention than they are with any product that might bring them money by conventional means. This is a sadly dysfunctional situation that has gripped and diminished the entire field of psychiatry as it struggles to protect the giant money that flows from the sales of its SSRIs and looks away from the country's opiate morass for fear of giving ketamine a shred of respectability.

That this situation is a disgrace to all those caught up in its web is without question, but this topic is discussed adequately elsewhere in this book and in other writings. In this brief writing I would like to discuss where ketamine, SSRIs and psychiatry will be in 5 to 10 years.

At this moment Big Pharma and the academic medical establishment – what is often referred to as the "Medical-Industrial Complex" - holds most of the cards but is seeing steady erosion of its power. SSRIs, the mainstay of psychiatry's approach to depression, produce billions in cash flow. The pharmaceutical industry's maintenance of this position is dependent upon three things:

1. The momentum of the huge cash-SSRI flow, present now for the past 20 years.
2. The willingness of insurance companies to continue to support a product that is demonstrably inferior to the ketamine which insurance companies only minimally recognize.
3. The continued lack of public clarity regarding ketamine's marked safety and effectiveness which is dependent both upon Big Pharma's suppression of ketamine and the insurance company's willingness to allow Big Pharma to tell it how to think.

There are four major players in America's current depression- defined mental health crisis:

1. Big Pharma and academia standing behind their SSRIs and SNRIs.
2. Clinics of Ketamine and the caregivers populating them.
3. Insurance companies.
4. The depressed, the anxious and those of PTSD, including our vets and, perhaps most significantly, our anxiety-ridden and depressed teens.

Big Pharma and Academia

Big Pharma is dependent upon money. Their primary source of revenue is the blockbuster drug, an entity in increasingly short supply. With revenues dropping, I see little likelihood that the pharmaceutical industry will release its grip on academia, find the blockbuster drugs that it needs to release its dependency on SSRIs, or simply doing the right thing by its citizenry by allowing ketamine to distribute its healing. As Joseph Lieberman's book *Shrinks* asserts, effective mental health drugs have never lent themselves to directed discovery; we are not likely to formulate another effective antidepressant of ketamine's caliber within the next 20 years.

Consequently, the Medical Industrial Complex will relentlessly juggernaut on like an Avengers movie written by Bernie Madoff.

Clinics of Ketamine

I confess to a bias of very high hope. People have heard of ketamine such that it would take massive and hurtful energies to get it back into the bottle. As the coverage of ketamine continues to expand, the validity of its success will translate to unstoppability, especially when we accept that our children are at stake.

Insurance Companies

Insurance companies should be able to serve as the unbiased observer standing between the forces of medical mental health effectiveness that is ketamine, and the forces of medical bottom-line obsession that is the Medical-Industrial Complex.

A few insurance companies are allegedly reimbursing for varieties of ketamine treatment. This refocus on illness rather than bottom-line

integrity could be the element that most effectively gets ketamine to the people that need it, namely the depressed, the anxious and those of PTSD, including our vets and, perhaps most significantly, our anxious and depressed teens.

As mentioned elsewhere, the iGens, or teens, are flaming into depression like an Australian bushfire. We have no measure of this unique level of depression, and the medical establishment has provided no acceptable explanation for the extreme ease of capitulation that has been rendered by virtually every teen.

My personal feelings are that even discussing this issue with academia and big Pharma has been made exceedingly difficult by the rearing of the "ugly head of the effectiveness of ketamine as viewed by the bottom-line forces of the SSRI-dependent Medical-Industrial Complex."

For America, and especially its youth, this is not a happy moment. And even a multiplying of the reach of ketamine by a factor of 10 or even 100 will not adequately address the problem. That being the case, if we looked a little bit less at the immediate future and even less at the screen of our smart phones, we might find a moment and a man for productive inspiration, where "the silent influence of character on character... in the contemplation of the lives of the great and good of the past," might influence tomorrow.

Sir William Osler could be that guy.

Sir William Osler

Sir William Osler died almost exactly one century ago. In a recent New England Journal of Medicine article, "Osler is revered for his efforts to place clinical medicine on a rational foundation." He spoke of a productive "Chauvinism in Medicine" and listed four "great features of the guild" that include:

1. Noble ancestry.
2. Remarkable solidarity.
3. Progressive character.
4. Singular beneficence.

The first of these is a thing of local culture, but the next three I would assert to be exceedingly mixed in their purity. Twenty years later Osler found himself equally compromised in his praise during a speech shortly after the Great War in which he himself had lost a son and many close friends. He expressed a special hope that we can relate to today in which the Hippocratic oath's implied love of humanity would combine with its love of craft to find a special wisdom that would direct science to be a force for good rather than evil.

Osler referred to "the profession of medicine as "a remarkable world unit" that offered a "fuller hope for humanity than in any other direction."

We, of course, all hope that Sir Osler's hopes hold sway in these equally pressing and compromised of times.

BIBLIOGRAPHY

1. Abbot, Alison. "What Animals Really Think." Nature Vol 584(13 August 2020) 183:185.
2. Bianco, Isaac H., and Stephen W. Wilson. "The habenular nuclei: a conserved asymmetric relay station in the vertebrate brain." *Philosophical Transactions of the Royal Society* 364 (4 December 2008): 1005-1020.
3. Binswanger, Ingrid. "Opioid Use Disorder and Incarceration – Hope for Ensuring the Continuity of Treatment." *New England Journal of Medicine* 380:13 (March 28, 2019): 1193-1195.
4. Bourdain, Anthony. *Kitchen Confidential: Adventures in the Culinary Underbelly.* Harper Collins, 195 Broadway, New York 2000.
5. Bryan, Charles S., M.D. and Scott H. Podolsky, M.D. "Sir William Ostler (1849-1919) – The Uses of History and the Singular Beneficence of Medicine." *New England Journal of Medicine* 381 (2019): 2194-2196.
6. Calderone, Ana. "The Ride of a Lifetime." In *Time Mental Health Special Edition,* edited by Edward Felthenthal. New York: Meredith Corporation, 2019: 22-26.
7. Calabrese, Lori. "Titrated Serial Ketamine Infusions Stop Outpatient Suicidality and Avert ER Visits and Hospitalizations." *International Journal of Psychiatry Research* Vol 2, no. 5 (September 2019): 1-12.
8. Cote, Charles, I. David Todres, Nishan G. Goudsouzian, John F.Ryan. *A Practice of Anesthesia for Infants and Children, 4th Edition.* Saunders, 2009.
9. Della Volpe, John. "Instagram has negatively impacted social relationships, according to new youth pole." www.msnbc.com/morningjoe. September 20, 2021.
10. Dwyer, Kate. "6 Critical Risks Facing the Pharmaceutical Industry." (June 29, 2018): (http://riskandinsurance.com/author/katie-dwyer).
11. Gardner, Caleb, and Arthur Kleinman. "Medicine and the Mind – The Consequences of Psychiatry's Identity Crisis." *New England Journal of Medicine* 381:18 (October 31, 2019): 1697-1699.

12. Gargeya, Rishab. *Osmind Data Report for Ketamine SLC.* Salt Lake City, September 2, 2020.
13. Gessen, Masha. "The Dying Russians." *The New York Review of Books I* (September 2, 2014).
14. Greenberg, Gary. "Psychiatry's Incurable Hubris." *The Atlantic* (April 2019).
15. Harrington, Anne. *The Mind Fixers.* New York: W.W. Norton & Co., Inc., 2019.
16. Heid, Markham. "The Loneliness Epidemic. In *Time Mental Health Special Edition,* edited by Edward Felthenthal, 16-21. New York: Meredith Corporation, 2019.
17. Hunter, David J., M.B., B.S., ScD. "The Complementarity of Public Health and Medicine – Achieving 'the Highest Attainable Standard of Health.'" *New England Journal of Medicine* 381:6 (August 5, 2021): 481-484.
18. Hyde, Stephen. "ketamine for Depression." Xlibris, 2015.
19. Jha, Manash, Bruce D. Grannemann, Joseph M. Trombello, E. Will Clark, Sara Levinson Eidelman, Tiffany Lawson, Tracy L. Greer, A. John Rush, and Madhukar H. Trivedi. "A Structured Approach to Detecting and Treating Depression in Primary Care: VitalSign6 Project." *The Annals of Family Medicine* 17, no. 4 (July 2019) 326-335. DOI: https://doi.org/10.1370/afm.2418.
20. Lieberman, Jeffrey A., M.D., with Ogi Ogas. *Shrinks The Untold Story of Psychiatry.* New York: Little, Brown and Company, March 2015.
21. Marques, Joao C., Meng Li, Diane Schaak, Drew N. Robson, and Jennifer M. Li. "Internal State Dynamics Shape Brain-Wide Activity and Foraging Behavior." *Nature* (December 18,2019).
22. Merriam-Webster. "Merriam-Webster's Collegiate Dictionary Eleventh Edition." Faridabad: Thompson Press India Ltd, May 2020.
23. Mylan Institutional. *Ketamine Hydrochloride Injection, USP* Mylan Institutional LLC, August 2018.
24. Oaklander, Mandy. "A Toll on Doctors." In Time Mental Health Special Edition, edited by Edward Felthenthal, 32-39. New York: Meredith Corporation, 2019.
25. Orwell, George. *A Collection of Essays.* New York: Houghton Mifflin Harcourt Publishing, 1981.
26. Platt, Craig W. "Beneath the Furrowed Brow: A Ketamine Journey in the ER." *Anesthesiology* Vol 125 (2016) 599-601.

27. Podolsky, Scott H., M.D., David Herzberg, Ph.D., and Jeremy A. Greene, M.D., PhD. "Preying on Prescribers (and Their Patients) – Pharmaceutical Marketing, Iatrogenic Epidemics, and the Sackler Legacy." *New England Journal of Medicine* Vol 380, no 19. (May 9,2019): 1785-1787.
28. Pollan, Michael. *How to Change Your Mind.* New York: Penguin Press, 2018.
29. Rantala, Markus, Severi Luoto, Indrikus Krams, Hasse Karlsson. "Depression Subtyping Based on Evolutionary Psychiatry: Proximate Mechanisms and Ultimate Functions." *Brain, Behavior, and Immunity* 69 (March 2018): 603-607.
30. Reilly, Katie. "Depression on Campus." In *Time Mental Health Special Edition,* edited by Edward Felthenthal, 28-31.
31. Rosenbaum, S., J.D., and D.R. Hawkins, Jr., B.A. The Good Doctor: Jack Geiger, Social Justice, and U.S. Health Policy." *New England Journal of Medicine* 384:11 (March, 18 2021): 983-985.
32. Shorter, Edward. *A History of Psychiatry* New York: John Wiley & Sons, Inc. 1997.
33. Sinclair, Upton. *The Jungle* Double Day, Page & Co. February 26, 1906.
34. Solomon, Andrew. *The Noonday Demon.* New York: Simon & Shuster, May 2015.
35. Tamouza, Ryad, Rajagopal Krishnamoorthy, Marion Leboyer. "Understanding the genetic contribution of the human leukocyte antigen system to common major psychiatric disorders in a world pandemic context." *Brain, Behavior, and Immunity* Vol 91 (05 October 2020): 731-739.
36. Treston, Greg. "What is the nature of the emergence phenomenon when using intravenous or intramuscular ketamine for procedural sedation?" *Emergency Medicine Australasia* (September 2009): 315-322.
37. Yang, Yan, Yihui Cui, Kangning Sang, Yiyan Dong, Zheyi Ni, Shuangshuang Ma, and Hailan Hu. "Ketamine blocks bursting in the lateral habenula to rapidly relieve depression." *Nature* Vol 554 (15 February 2018): 317-322.
38. Zeng, Tian Chen, Alan J. Aw, Marcus W. Feldman. "Cultural Hitchhiking and competition between patrilineal kin groups explain the post-Neolithic Y-chromosome bottleneck." *Nature Communications* Vol. 9, no. 2077 (May 2018)

www.ingramcontent.com/pod-product-compliance
Lightning Source LLC
LaVergne TN
LVHW051926051126
851857LV00020B/2043

* 9 7 9 8 9 5 2 0 3 0 3 2 9 *